Becoming a
Professional Tutor
in the Lifelong Learning Sector

Becoming a
Professional Tutor
in the Lifelong Learning Sector

Jonathan Tummons

LearningMatters

First published in 2007 by Learning Matters Ltd

British Library Cataloguing in Publication Data
A CIP record for this book is available from the British Library.

ISBN: 978 1 84445 077 0

Cover design by Topics – The Creative Partnership
Project management by Deer Park Productions, Tavistock, Devon
Typeset by PDQ Typesetting Ltd
Printed and bound in Great Britain by Bell & Bain Ltd, Glasgow

Learning Matters Ltd
33 Southernhay East
Exeter EX1 1NX
Tel: 01392 215560
Email: info@learningmatters.co.uk
www.learningmatters.co.uk

Contents

The author

Jonathan Tummons

Jonathan Tummons is a lecturer in teacher training at York College, a member of the Consortium for Post-Compulsory Education and Training. Prior to this he taught for ten years at the School of Continuing Education at the University of Leeds and has wide experience of working with adult learners for other universities and for the Workers' Educational Association. As a consultant he has contributed to programmes for schools broadcast by Channel 4. Jonathan is currently engaged in postgraduate research, funded by the ESRC, at Lancaster University, and is a fellow of the Institute of Learning.

Acknowledgements

The author and publisher would like to thank the following for permission to reproduce copyright material:

Taylor and Francis Ltd. (www.tandf.co.uk/journals)
The National Institute for Adult and Continuing Education

Every effort has been made to trace the copyright holders and to obtain their permission for the use of copyright material. The publisher and author will gladly receive any information enabling them to rectify any error or omission in subsequent editions.

Acknowledgements

I should like to thank a number of people who, even though they may not know it, have contributed to the thought processes that ended up in this book.

So, hello and thanks to: John Aston, Suzanne Blake, Jane Brooke, Jennifer Clark, David Dearing, Roy Fisher, Jacki Gill, Nick Haigh, Laura Kent, Mary Hamilton, David Lamburn, Chris Letza, Julie Mayo, Anne Metcalfe, Jayne Moore, Gaynor Mount, David Neve, Dean Starkey, Ron Thompson, and especially, as always, Jo.

And a final thank you to my son, even though he is too young to read this (or anything else, for that matter). Without him, this book would have been written a lot more quickly, but with a lot less fun in between the word processing. So this book is for Alex.

Introduction

This book is intended to help all those who are currently working towards a teaching qualification that is accredited by Lifelong Learning UK (LLUK). You may already be working as a teacher or trainer in a further education (FE) college, and studying for your professional qualifications on a part-time, in-service basis. Alternatively, you may be studying for your qualification on a full-time basis, and may be about to embark on, or already engaged on, a teaching placement. You may be employed, or seeking employment, as a tutor in adult or community education, provided by a local education authority or by organisations such as the Workers' Educational Association (WEA). You may be working as a trainer or instructor in the health sector, or in the police or fire services. These varied contexts are all covered by the LLUK Standards, and practitioners in these areas are all eligible for LLUK accreditation.

This is not primarily a theoretical work. Professionalism, the nature of professional work and of professional expertise, are subjects of considerable theoretical and research-based work: this book is not intended to be part of that particular body of literature. However, there are a few occasions when a focus on current research is desirable, and the references provided will allow those with a taste for theory to explore further. Essentially, this book is intended to provoke action as well as thought: the activities within this book, often underpinned by case studies which are composite forms of real-life experiences that I have encountered in adult education centres, further education colleges and in community-based education and training settings, are designed to facilitate the application of the ideas and issues discussed in the real world of the teacher or trainer.

Meeting National Standards

From 1 January 2005 a new organisation, Lifelong Learning UK, began operating as the body responsible for – among other things – the professional development of all employees in the field of lifelong learning. LLUK is responsible for the new occupational standards that are at the heart of this book. A more detailed account of the role of LLUK can be found in Chapter 3.

How to use this book

This book may be read from cover to cover, in one sitting, or it may be read on a chapter-by-chapter basis over a longer period of time. Each chapter is designed so that it can be read in isolation, as and when needed, although references to topics covered in other chapters will be found from time to time.

Within each chapter, the reader will find a number of features that are designed to engage the reader and provoke an active response to the ideas and themes that are covered. Objectives at the start of each chapter set the scene, and then the appropriate LLUK Professional Standards for that chapter are listed. In many places, an activity will be found. These activities have been designed to facilitate the practical application of some of the issues covered. Similarly, a range of focus activities is also included. Some of the focus activities are designed to draw attention to certain details; others are designed to stimulate reflection and debate; and some are designed to draw attention to some current and recent debates in educational theory and research, as they relate to professionalism. The case studies and real-life examples that are to be found in this book are drawn from a variety of different teaching and training contexts, as a reflection of the diversity of the learning and skills sector as a whole. Finally, each chapter concludes with suggestions for what to do next. A small number of sources, books, journal articles and websites, are recommended at the end of each chapter. These lists are by no means exhaustive. Featured items have been chosen because of their suitability and value for use and study by trainee teachers in the learning and skills sector.

Learning, and reading this book

My own research is focused on how trainee teachers in the learning and skills sector make sense of the assessment requirements that they have to meet while studying for their teacher training qualifications. From this perspective, as well as from my perspective as a teacher educator, I have radically changed my own ideas about what I think learning is, and how it can be made to happen. This book is not an appropriate venue for me to set forth my own views, but one or two comments are, I feel, necessary. Firstly, a general point: I think that learning can happen in all kinds of places and at all kinds of times, and it never really stops. Learning happens as a consequence of our social actions: talking to colleagues or friends; going to work; finding ways to deal with dilemmas that we have not encountered before. In this book, I have tried to set out some themes and ideas that can be quite remote and theoretical, and to situate them firmly within the working lives of tutors.

Secondly, a more specific point: I think that language needs to be used carefully. There is a lot of jargon in teacher education and despite my efforts and assurances, many of the trainees with whom I have worked still resist it. In this book, I have tried to cut the use of jargon to a minimum. There is a place for it: the right words can say in a small amount of space what might otherwise take a long time. There are also, in teacher education, a number of books and articles that are sometimes a little daunting to the reader, especially to those for whom teacher training is a first experience of higher education (HE). I have tried to keep this reader in mind, while at the same time providing sufficient depth for the more academically experienced reader. Many of the trainees that I meet have a particular bugbear: Harvard referencing. At some points in the text, I have deliberately avoided Harvard conventions, although all suggestions for further reading – books and journal articles – are in the correct style.

I am always happy to hear from trainee teachers about my writing or my research and to receive offers from trainees who would be willing to help. My email address is j.tummons@lancaster.ac.uk

1
The classroom and the college

By the end of this chapter you should:

- **have a developing understanding of debates relating to the professionalism of tutors in the learning and skills sectors;**
- **be aware of some of the roles performed by tutors in a professional capacity;**
- **have a developing understanding of the ways in which professionalism is defined.**

Professional Standards

This chapter does not relate to any specific Professional Standards.

Getting down to work

This chapter is called 'the classroom and the college', for reasons of simplicity if nothing else. The learning and skills sector is remarkable in its diversity (I am pretty sure that people who work in other educational sectors, such as primary schools or universities, don't quite realise how wide the sector is) and this chapter could easily have been called 'the workshop, classroom, office, computer suite or construction site, and the college, adult education building, outreach centre or family learning centre'. The point is that in the learning and skills sector, the work of tutors (who might also be called trainers, instructors, facilitators or teachers) and learners (who might also be called trainees, students, apprentices or candidates) happens in all sorts of places and at all sorts of times. There are full-time and part-time courses. Some part-time courses are held during the day, others in the evening. Some learners are in employment, others are not. Some learners are enrolled on programmes of study or training that have a direct relevance to their job; for others, attendance at college might be a step towards a new job; and for others, attendance at college might be the first step of a longer learning journey after starting a family. Some tutors are full-time, others are part-time. Some part-time tutors may rarely meet their full-time colleagues; others are more fully involved in the life of the organisation in which they work; and others perform a training role alongside a broader operational role within an organisation.

Put simply, there is no such thing as a standard job role in the learning and skills sector: it is a tremendously varied environment. Some tutors will spend their working lives in a classroom with tables and chairs, a data projector for their PowerPoint presentations and a pile of portfolios to assess once a term or so. Other tutors will work in poorly furnished rooms in outreach centres, with an old overhead projector beamed onto a wall because there isn't a screen.

REFLECTIVE TASK

Before reading on, spend some time thinking about the other members of your teacher training group. You may be working towards a professional qualification on a part-time basis, in which case you and your fellow trainees will already be working on a part-time or full-time basis. Where do you all work? What are the different subject areas that are represented within your group? What kinds of learner do you all work with – what age are they, and what are their backgrounds? If you are working towards your professional qualification on a full-time basis, you may be about to go on a placement, or you may have already done so. Talk to the other members of your teacher training group about the different colleges and departments that you have spent time in.

Even within a single institution, diversity is easy to find. The look and feel of a business studies classroom is quite different from the look and feel of a plumbing workshop, but they may only be a few dozen yards apart. And the bustle of the plumbing workshop will feel very different again from the quiet space of an adult numeracy session, which in turn will be different again from a one-to-one session where a learning support tutor is providing additional study support to a learner for whom English is not their first language. With such diversity in the sector, it may seem to be folly to try to write a single book that encompasses the professional lives of so many different kinds of tutor. But in fact, there are many common themes and issues running through these very different contexts and places for learning.

Being professional

What does it mean to be 'professional?' For that matter, what does it mean to be 'unprofessional'? Who gets to decide what counts as professional or unprofessional behaviour, and on what grounds? Why is it that some occupations are described as professions and others are not? And why, perhaps most importantly, do tutors working in the learning and skills sector need to worry about all these issues?

The last question needs answering first, and the answer needs to move beyond a merely instrumental answer that would say something like:

> *You need to know about these issues because they are in the teacher training syllabus, and before you are given your Cert Ed (Certificate in Education), you will have to do an assignment on this topic.*

This is indeed the case, but it's hardly satisfactory. A better answer might be:

> *You need to know about these issues because they make up a large part of the professional standards that all tutors in the learning and skills sector have to work towards.*

This is perhaps a little more helpful: in the introduction to this book, the development of the new LLUK standards, replacing the Further Education National Training Organisation (Fento) standards, was explained in the context of the development of new professional qualifications for the sector. But there's still a tone of compulsion at work, something that has to be done rather than something that has been chosen. Another answer might be:

> *You need to know about these issues because they will help you, as a tutor, to make sense of some of the things that you experience during your working day.*

Perhaps this is more useful. After all, both new and experienced tutors often encounter things that make them stop in their tracks for a moment. It might be an admissions policy that doesn't seem to make sense ('Surely this learner would be better off somewhere else? They don't have the right prior qualifications for this course, so why am I being pressured to take them on?') Or it might be the behaviour of a learner or group of learners ('They only turn up at all because they get their £30 a week. Why are they here if they have no real interest in what I'm trying to get them to do?').

> *You need to know about these issues because there is so much more to being a tutor than just doing some teaching. In order to do justice to the job, you need to know about why the job is done the way that it is, and who shapes that job description.*

Being a tutor in the learning and skills sector is an ever-changing job (or should that be 'an ever-changing profession'?) Government legislation leads to changes in the curricula that we have to teach. Changing attitudes mean that we now work with a much more diverse learner population. New funding regimes mean that we have to work towards different targets each year. So perhaps all these answers help explain the relevance of an exploration of issues surrounding professionalism to the learning and skills tutor. But this still hasn't helped us to work out what professionalism is, or whether being a tutor is a profession.

Profession or vocation?

Historically, some occupations have been classed as professions and others as vocations. The word 'vocation' derives from the Latin word *vocare*, which means 'to call', and an occupation that is a vocation is, literally, a calling, the kind of job that someone chooses to do because they have a sense of being called to do it by some kind of sense of purpose or duty or selfless obligation. Traditionally, becoming a priest has long been seen as a vocation. Becoming a nurse used to be seen as a vocation, but is more often thought of as a profession these days: and it may not be a coincidence that as nursing has become a profession instead of a vocation, nurses increasingly access higher education in order to gain appropriate qualifications. Originally, professions were seen as being distinct from vocations, and from other occupations that might be thought of as unskilled or not requiring mental or intellectual effort. Five hundred years ago, doctors and lawyers were seen as professionals; skilled artisans such as silversmiths or stonemasons were not. Today, people still talk about the medical profession or the legal profession, but we would not describe a stonemason or an electrician as being members of a profession. However, it is quite possible that, having seen an electrician do a really good job when rewiring a house, he might be described as 'having done a really professional job'. And just to add to the confusion, a vocation no longer refers to a calling such as the priesthood. In the learning and skills sector, distinctions are often made between the academic curriculum and the vocational curriculum, the latter referring to technical, manual or practical activity.

The next step is to re member, therefore, that there is some kind of distinction between a profession, and being professional. There are a number of different theoretical approaches to defining a profession, in fact, and these will be explored in depth in Chapter 6. But they are worth referring to at this stage. Briefly, and combining a number of different theoretical perspectives, a profession can be defined as possessing a number of characteristics, including:

- **a theoretical knowledge on which practical or skill-based activity rests;**
- **formal, accredited qualifications, awarded by an approved provider, which provide a grounding in the theoretical knowledge required;**

- a licence to practise, or some other public proof of occupational competence, normally acquired through examination;
- a code of professional conduct or practice;
- a professional body that represents the interests of practitioners, and regulates their activity in some way;
- some kind of concern as to the impact or consequences of the actions of members of the profession.

So one way of thinking about being a professional is the extent to which an occupation meets – or doesn't meet – these six characteristics.

Behaving in an unprofessional manner

There are other ways of thinking about being professional that don't simply equate to the status attached to an occupation. If an electrician can be said to have done a professional job, and yet not be described as a professional, then the meaning of the word must be more flexible than just adhering to some abstract characteristics of the kind listed above. And it works the other way round. If a tutor swore at a learner, such behaviour might be described as unprofessional. If a painter and decorator left a tremendous mess behind after decorating a house, that might be seen as unprofessional as well. Someone can be described as unprofessional without being a member of a profession. So where do these broader definitions come from?

In part, of course, being unprofessional is the exact opposite of being professional. So if a member of a profession which possesses the six characteristics listed above acts in a manner opposite to one of those characteristics, then that would be an example of unprofessional behaviour. A professional acting in breach of a profession's code of conduct would be a straightforward example.

The unprofessional tutor (i)

LLUK Professional Standard AK5.2 states that tutors know and understand:

The need for confidentiality in communicating with others about learners.

A tutor on a work-based learning programme who divulged information about a learner's progress to another member of the same group would unambiguously be acting against the interests of the learners in question and would be in breach of AP2 (v).

Different professions have different codes of practice or conduct to work towards, and where such codes come from, and how they are made to work, are explored in detail in Chapter 5. But it is possible to describe a pattern of behaviour as unprofessional without detailed knowledge of a profession's code of practice.

The unprofessional tutor (ii)

LLUK Professional Standard AP6.2 states that tutors should:

Demonstrate good practice through maintaining a learning environment which conforms to statutory requirements.

A tutor working with a group of 14–16 year old learners at a further education college who did not carry out a pre-visit inspection and then failed to provide proper supervision during an off-site visit, leading to one of

---

the learners being involved in an accident, would be in breach of this standard. However, the parent or guardian of the young person in question, or of any of the members of the group, might not even be aware of the existence of the LLUK professional standards, let alone this specific clause. And yet the tutor in question would, unhesitatingly, be accused of being unprofessional in failing to provide adequate supervision.

Definitions of what constitutes professional and unprofessional behaviour can readily be found outside dictionaries or teacher-training textbooks; and they can be found in the real world, in the attitudes and opinions of tutors, learners, parents and guardians, or other stakeholders. Some aspects of professional behaviour are common across different contexts: it is never acceptable, for example, to use sexist language. Other aspects of professional behaviour are more variable: dress codes, for example, vary between different occupations or, in a college context, between different departments. A learner on a beauty therapy course who forgets to wear whites might be told to go back home and change, or might be warned that if they arrived incorrectly dressed at college the next day, they would be told to go home. By contrast, Cert Ed or PGCE (Post Graduate Certificate in Education) classes tend to be less strict in setting guidelines for dress.

The professional tutor at work

This chapter, then, is an exploration of what it means to be a professional tutor, within the confines of a place of work which might be a large further education college, a small community education building or an industry-based setting. And the following discussion rests on a number of assumptions. The issues raised apply to all tutors in the learning and skills sector, and it doesn't matter:

- **if you are full-time or part-time;**
- **which curriculum area you work in, or what kinds of learners you work with;**
- **if you have nearly finished your teacher training, or if you completed your teacher training several years ago;**
- **if you are a member of a professional body such as the Institute for Learning, or not;**
- **whether or not you are a member of a trade union, such as the UCU.**

Some aspects of professional behaviour are – it is hoped – so commonplace that they only need a very brief mention. So a list of exemplary forms of professionalism might start off with the following.

- **Knowing your subject.**
- **Arriving on time and being fully prepared for a teaching or training session.**
- **Keeping to deadlines, for example, when marking and returning assignments to learners.**
- **Using appropriate language when talking with learners.**
- **Treating all learners the same.**
- **Modelling best practice: conducting work in a manner that learners should be willing to try to emulate.**

Statements such as these are quite generic, and easily transfer to other occupational contexts. If the word 'learners' is replaced by the word 'clients', then the applicability of such statements to other professions becomes apparent (and it is also worth remembering that in many senses, learners are clients or customers). However, the learning and skills workplace is a complex one, shaped and swayed by a range of forces such as government policy, the concerns of employers and the target setting of funding bodies. There are aspects of the role of the tutor that make up quite distinct components of a professional approach to the role, and these are not always easily agreed upon. The different people who work in the sector – tutors, managers, support workers – do not always see eye to eye on everything; nor will they always be in agreement with those stakeholders who are not immediately involved in education or training, but who have considerable influence, such as government ministers or employers. It is arguably in these areas of tension that the limits of professionalism are established.

CASE STUDY CASE STUDY CASE STUDY CASE STUDY CASE STUDY CASE STUDY

The first session of the year

As you read through the following case study, think about how the issues raised are managed in the college or training centre in which you work. Have you been involved in a similar situation? If you are not working as a tutor, but are on – or are about to take up – a teaching placement, talk to colleagues about whether or not these issues have applied to them. And talk to your mentor as well.

It is the start of a new year at a busy college of further education. September is always a very busy time because of enrolment and admissions. There is a lot of paperwork involved (which can be frustrating in itself) and a lot of rushing around with interviews, finding classrooms, preparing resources and so on. It is not that common for new tutors to have a responsibility for admissions onto a course, but it does happen. On some courses, the admissions process is completed at an early stage, perhaps over the summer. Other courses carry on recruiting until the very last minute, especially if there are financial considerations: after all, if a class is too small, it will lose money and probably have to close.

The overall number of learners in a class is determined by a number of factors, some of which are quite practical. A carpentry and joinery workshop might contain only 14 workbenches, so a class of 19 learners might cause problems when it comes to practical work. A teaching room might contain 18 chairs and tables, all arranged in such a way that everyone can see the data projection screen and whiteboard, so a class of 27 learners might be a tight squeeze, especially if the room is only just big enough for 18. Other factors relating to ideal class size might be determined by the approaches taken by tutors. For a lecture-style session, it is perfectly possible to accommodate a large group – 80 or 90, even. Such approaches are seldom used in further education, however. An adult education group might need to recruit 10 learners in order to be financially viable, but if there were more than 16 in the group, the tutor might have to change his or her teaching style: it is difficult to run a discussion group, or seminar, with a large number of learners because not everyone will be able to take part. Nonetheless, targets for recruitment are normally set at the start of each academic year, and managers and resource coordinators do take into account things such as room size, time of day and the nature of the course.

You are the tutor on an accredited foreign language class. Recruitment is good – so good, in fact, that you have 28 learners booked in to your class. Normally, the room that you use could hold 20. If recruitment hits 30, then college policy dictates that the class could be split into two groups of 15. In fact, this will not happen as your manager has let you know that the department would not be able to afford another tutor. As well as having to rush around preparing extra handouts at the last minute, you will have to work in a very crowded room, and there is no chance of transferring to a larger room for at least six weeks. On the first day of the course, two more learners turn up, hoping

> **to join the class at the last minute. And you are in no doubt that they would be greatly disappointed if they were turned away.**

There are a number of issues arising here.

1. The number of learners in the group
This looks like being quite a large group. Notwithstanding the fact that one or two may drop out during the year (and a certain rate of learner drop-out is perhaps inevitable), a group this size will need managing and planning for quite differently from a group of 15: learning and teaching strategies and resources may need revising; the classroom furniture will have to be arranged in a different pattern; there will be more assignments to mark. And this all impacts on

2. The tutor's workload
The tutor now has a lot more work to do: extra preparation; extra marking; redesigning the scheme of work to take account of the different activities that will need to be employed. The sheer quantity of paperwork involved constitutes a meaningful time commitment: application forms; registration; library cards and computer network passwords; organising induction. Then again, it rather balances out what happened the year before, when one of the tutors' classes was allowed to run even though the official recruitment target had not been met. And the status of the tutor is an issue here. If the tutor is only on an hourly-paid contract, then the amount of preparation needed for each of those hours can be seen as an additional burden. Then again, if the tutor is a full-time member of staff, the work still needs to be done. And this all impacts on

3. Available resources
Getting some extra handouts produced is not too much of a problem. Working in a room which is too small for such large group is. Partly this is due to sheer physical discomfort: a crowded room can get hot, stuffy and noisy. But there is also a pedagogical impact: in order to get all the learners in, it may not be possible to arrange the furniture so that there are clear, open sightlines between the tutor and the learners, and between the learners themselves. A smaller class is easy to move around the room, to split up and then reconvene when changing from small-group work to plenary work. And it might be tempting to blame

4. College admissions policy
In fact, irrespective of the admissions policy of the college, it would be highly questionable for a tutor to turn away a learner just for want of a chair for them to sit at, unless health and safety issues were involved. A more forceful argument could be made if the oversubscribed class was in a construction or engineering block, rather than modern languages. Extra resources for a language class are quite easily arranged: extra resources for a vehicle engineering class that has almost doubled in size in comparison to last year are of a different magnitude in every sense of the word.

Summing up

Issues such as these are locally variable: that is to say, different institutions will always have their own ways of doing things. Factors such as the availability of staff, the money needed to buy resources, the targets for recruitment agreed between a college and a funding body can all vary according to the size and geographical location of a college, or the demographic make-up of the community from which learners come.

CASE STUDY CASE STUDY CASE STUDY CASE STUDY CASE STUDY CASE STUDY

More than just teaching and training

Before moving on, spend some time thinking about all the different roles and responsibilities that make up your working life as a tutor, apart from actual teaching. What are the other aspects of your job? What else do you have to spend time and energy doing that are not necessarily related to classroom practice? If you are working towards your teaching qualification and have yet to take up a post, you might ask your mentor about their different responsibilities; or you might reflect on any relevant experiences that you might have had while on a teaching placement.

The summer term is always a busy period for tutors in further and adult education. As well as marking all those end-of-year assignments, there is a lot of preparation to do in advance of the new academic year. The details of the course that you teach on need to be checked before they go into a prospectus that is delivered to local households. New information leaflets about the course need to be written. Enrolment evenings, where prospective learners can find out more about the courses on offer, need to be arranged. And all of this takes time, especially when there is so much marking to be done. And there is little time to do it all: assignments need to be internally second-marked and then need to go for external verification.

Unsurprisingly, Paul, who is a full-time tutor, is feeling under pressure. Marking is taking up all his time. And when he is asked by his manager if he has completed the publicity materials that he has been asked for, the answer is 'No'. He has to do all the marking and complete lots of end-of-year paperwork as well: the learners' results need recording and submitting to both the college exam-inations office and to the awarding body, and a course report needs writing. Nor has Paul yet volunteered to attend one of the enrolment evenings. Paul's line manager does sympathise with him over the volume of work that he has to do, but points out that many other tutors are in the same position and he is expected to comply. Paul is not mollified by this, and feels that he is being asked to do too many things that shouldn't really be his responsibility in the first place. The college has a marketing department. Why can't they sort it out? It's not as if he is being given time off from his marking, or his other teaching duties, in order to help with the publicity. His line manager simply shrugs his shoulders, and tells Paul that if one of the courses does not recruit, then he will have to do some teaching on a different course as well, perhaps for another department.

Much of the work that a tutor has to do is related to learning and teaching: preparing learning resources; liaising with external examiners; marking assignments and recording the results. And then there are all those things that don't really seem to be related to learning and teaching at all, such as taking part in marketing and publicity activities. If the college has a marketing department, staffed (presumably) by people who have qualifications and experi-ence in sales or marketing, why do tutors, with qualifications and experience related to the subject that they teach, have to spend so much time advertising these courses?

Of course, it is in the interests of all tutors that their course should recruit sufficient numbers of learners. For part-time hourly-paid tutors, a high level of recruitment is a pressing issue of financial security for the forthcoming year. Taking all this into consideration, surely spending some time and effort on making sure that numbers are good is a kind of investment? Moreover, if recruitment was low and a course was cancelled, a tutor might find him/herself being asked to teach a different course instead: a course that he/she might not have taught before and may not be particularly well qualified to teach.

There are two quite distinct issues relating to professional identity at work here:

1. the idea that professionalism is based on a specific area of theoretical, vocational or technical expertise, acquired through education and training;
2. the idea that a professional's role is tightly circumscribed by that specialist knowledge and training.

As far as Paul is concerned, his job is to teach. He has a degree in sports science and a range of coaching qualifications. He trains exercise professionals in the sport and leisure industry, and he likes to think that he is good at his job: his learners' achievement results would certainly back him up. He grumbles about the amount of paperwork that is involved, but then again so do many other teachers in the learning and skills sector (and in the primary and secondary sectors as well). But he is not qualified in marketing. Why, when other people are qualified and experienced in this field, does he have to get involved? In one respect, Paul is fortunate: he is a permanent member of staff, and even if he has to do some teaching in a different department, his post is still secure. For a part-time tutor, the situation is considerably more risky: a part-timer might feel particularly pressured to invest time and effort in recruitment activities, because their income is on the line. Unsurprisingly, many part-time tutors find this period of the academic year to be a stressful one.

If Paul is to be defined as a professional, then this definition of professionalism needs to be thought about in the light of the characteristics of professionalism that were put forward earlier in this chapter. Paul is expected to do work that is in no way connected to his occupational or theoretical competence or expertise, irrespective of the fact that there is an office full of professional marketers and publicists on the college grounds. He is being asked to put time and energy into recruitment, perhaps giving up two or three evenings so that he can help out at an enrolment event. And if he were to refuse to do so (although of course he can hardly do that) he would undoubtedly be accused of being unprofessional. So, if Paul's course does not recruit a sufficient number of learners, what then? As a full-time tutor, Paul has to teach for a certain number of hours during the academic year. If numbers are low in his curriculum area, then he may well find himself teaching on a programme which is unfamiliar to him. Indeed, many tutors in the learning and skills sector are employed on contracts that do not specify the exact subjects that they teach: flexibility at work is a standard condition of employment.

There are a number of questions to ask: what kind of profession does not necessarily rely on the expertise of the practitioner? What kind of profession routinely seeks to redeploy its members in occupational roles for which they may not be sufficiently well qualified or experienced? What kind of profession prides flexibility above expertise? Some tutors, like Paul, articulate their concerns. But at the end of the day, tutors are told that it is their responsibility to help with recruitment, and with any number of other activities that are not to do with learning and teaching.

Redefining professionalism

The ways in which definitions of 'profession' and 'professionalism' have changed over time have already been referred to in this chapter, as has the changing nature of some occupations that have only relatively recently acquired professional status. Moreover, some aspects of a working definition of professionalism have been suggested. Is being a teacher in the learning and skills sector a profession? Partly, of course, any answer to this will depend on how professionalism is defined. This is not an entirely straightforward exercise, and there is a significant body of research relating to issues of professionalism in the learning and skills workplace which is explored in Chapter 6.

One or two issues have come to light in this chapter. Is a tutor in the learning and skills sector more of a professional, or less of one, for having to do work in so many areas that he or she is not formally qualified or experienced to do? Is being a professional tutor just about the tutoring, the working with learners and the assessing, or is it also about helping out at open evenings and writing entries for prospectuses? Perhaps wondering about whether being a tutor is a profession or not simply misses the point, and what is really important is the realisation that needing to be flexible in the workplace, being willing to be redeployed and to do whatever the organisation wants a worker to do, is the everyday reality of lots of different people, not just tutors. Is being professional simply another way of saying that tutors need to do what their employers want them to do?

Becoming a professional tutor: towards a working definition of professionalism

A working definition of professionalism is by no means straightforward. Abstract, theoretical definitions, such as those explored in Chapter 6, undoubtedly help to focus discussion, but it may be a fool's errand to assume that there can be a single definition. Nonetheless, there are clearly aspects of the role of the tutor that are perceived as being the characteristics of a professional practitioner: by tutors themselves, by college managers, by other stakeholders. And the expectations and perceptions of other stakeholders will be explored in the next chapter.

A SUMMARY OF **KEY POINTS**

In this chapter we have looked at a number of key themes:

> **The multifaceted role of the tutor.**

> **Patterns of professional and unprofessional behaviour in the workplace.**

> **Tensions in the workplace that affect the tutor's perception of their own role.**

Definitions of professionalism are in the eye of the beholder. And perhaps the most difficult issue that needs to be considered is the extent to which a working definition of professionalism in the learning and skills sector is used by a self-aware and confident body of tutors to define and circumscribe their practice, as against a working definition of professionalism shaped and codified by government legislation or college managers that is used to impose patterns of work on tutors. To put it another way, who owns definitions of professionalism in the learning and skills sector?

FURTHER READING FURTHER READING **FURTHER** READING FURTHER READING

Not all teacher training textbooks discuss issues relating to professionalism and professional values, and other more specialist works can be dense and offputting to the new reader. Two of the general textbooks that do include brief discussions of these themes are listed here.

Hillier, Y (2005) *Reflective teaching in further and adult education*, second edition. London: Continuum

Wallace, S (2005) *Teaching and supporting learning in further education*, second edition. Exeter: Learning Matters. Third edition due for publication in 2001.

Suggestions for more detailed further reading can be found at the end of Chapter 6.

2
Working in the Lifelong Learning Sector

By the end of this chapter you should:

- have developed an awareness of the influence of key stakeholders on professional practice in the learning and skills sector;
- have a critical understanding of the audit and inspection cultures at work within the sector;
- understand the role of quality assurance in the learning and skills sector;
- know some of the ways in which the tutor's professional practice is shaped by the demands of quality assurance.

Professional Standards

This chapter relates to the following Professional Standards:

Professional Values:

AS 7 Improving the quality of their practice.

Professional Knowledge and Understanding:

AK 7.1 Organisational systems and processes for recording learner information.

AK 7.2 Own role in the quality cycle.

AK 7.3 Ways to implement improvements based on feedback received.

Professional Practice:

AP 7.1 Keep accurate records which contribute to organisational procedures.

AP 7.2 Evaluate own contribution to the organisation's quality cycle.

AP 7.3 Use feedback to develop own practice within the organisation's systems.

The Lifelong Learning Sector: looking in

Every summer, when GCSE and A-level results are announced, schools hit the headlines, and not necessarily for the right reasons. Exams are, allegedly, getting easier, and teachers are always complaining about how much work they have to do. People's perceptions of schools and what goes on inside them, and their perceptions of the teachers who work in them, are shaped both by direct experience (being a parent) and through representations in the media. The same goes for universities. University lecturers went on strike in 2006 and refused to mark any students' work. In return, students threatened to sue universities if their degrees were delayed. So-called 'Mickey Mouse' degrees are vilified in the press. Three years ago, a proposed degree in surf and beach management had to be dropped by the Swansea Institute because nobody took the idea seriously, even though some students had already signed up.

These are grossly oversimplified issues, and of course the ways in which people form their ideas about schools or universities are far more complex than this. What is important is to realise that beyond the confines of a school or university, debates are always taking place about the work that is done by practitioners within those institutions. That is to say, within the sphere of public debate, ideas are formed about the professionalism of the people who work in these institutions. Simply by reading stories in the newspapers, people will form their opinions.

What do people outside the learning and skills sector see when they look in? Hopefully, they would see a busy, diverse setting for a range of different training and education opportunities, open to a diverse learner population. Adult education centres and colleges don't tend to hit the headlines quite as often as primary or secondary schools. But when they do, it provides an opportunity for thinking about the sector as a whole.

CLOSE FOCUS CLOSE FOCUS **CLOSE** FOCUS CLOSE FOCUS **CLOSE** FOCUS

Alan Johnson: more plumbing, less Pilates

Alan Johnson, MP for Kingston upon Hull West and Hessle, was appointed Secretary of State for Education and Skills in May 2006. The following month, he delivered a speech to the recently established Quality Improvement Agency for Lifelong Learning. A short extract of this speech was quickly reported in the media and stirred up a considerable debate:

We must rebalance taxpayers' money towards the subjects where there is greatest need – so more plumbing, less Pilates; subsidised precision engineering, not over-subsidised flower arranging, except of course where flower arranging is necessary for a vocational purpose.

Tai chi may be hugely valuable to people studying it, but it's of little value to the economy. There must be a fairer apportionment between those who gain from education and those who pay for it – state, employer or individual.

Surveys show that adults agree they should pay more for courses where they can.

So colleges shouldn't have to cut courses just because budgets in some areas have been reduced. The trick is making sure courses appeal to students and employers – keeping demand, interest and quality high. With these principles at the heart of a re-energised further education system, it is entirely possible for colleges to increase fees and raise enrolments at the same time.

Is this how people outside the learning and skills sector see it – as populated by adults on subsidised recreational evening classes and failing to provide enough opportunities for those seeking a vocational course?

In fact, this short quote from Alan Johnson's speech introduces a number of issues that have an impact on the professional role of the tutor.

1. What is the purpose of education and training in the learning and skills sector? Is it all about training people for the workplace, or are there other priorities as well?

It is important to remember that there are a lot of different stakeholders with an interest in what goes on in different parts of the learning and skills sector. Some stakeholders exert considerable influence: government ministers and funding bodies can, among other actions, target funding in certain areas at the expense of others. Some tutors find themselves teaching on courses which attract a considerable amount of public money. At the same time, they may well find themselves attracting a considerable amount of scrutiny: funding agencies will want to know how their money is being spent. This can lead to pressure. Basic and key skills classes undoubtedly attract more attention than a pottery class. And this might impact on the work of the tutor in a number of ways, in terms of monitoring of performance, of security of employment, and even in terms of the nature of the work that the tutor has to do: the more closely a course is monitored and audited, the greater the amount of paperwork.

Improving the literacy and numeracy levels of the adult population is undoubtedly an important goal in terms of up-skilling the workforce, combating social exclusion and providing opportunities for progression to further study. Next to this, the provision of a flower-arranging class might seem trivial at best. But those tutors who teach flower-arranging classes in adult education centres across England and Wales would beg to differ. Flower arranging as a subject might not be a priority for the workforce, but the softer outcomes of working with others, promoting social inclusion and encouraging participation in learning are not to be ignored.

2. What role do employers play in the learning and skills sector? What benefits do they derive from it?

A significant proportion of provision is undoubtedly directed at employment. This can work in a number of ways. Employers may allow employees to attend a programme of training at a college on a day-release basis, when employees need new skills or need to update existing ones. And while the exact arrangements will vary, it is important to remember that the cost to employers is far from negligible, in terms of both course fees and in the time needed to allow employees to attend. Day-release provision such as this can be found in a range of settings, from electrical engineers to hairdressers. Other learners in FE colleges access programmes of education and training before entering the workforce. Some programmes are delivered entirely within a college setting, while others include work-based placements.

The involvement of employers is entirely understandable, whether the focus is on individual employers or a trade association. Employers need to know that the courses that they send their employees on, or that they endorse, are fit for purpose: that they meet the requirements of a particular industry or trade. Alongside the Sector Skills Development Agency, Sector Skills Councils which represent, for example, environmental and land-based industries, or the retail motor industry, participate in the planning and designing of curricula, qualifications and provision of opportunities for education and training ranging from modern apprenticeships to foundation degrees.

3. What are the direct consequences of changes to the ways in which courses in the sector are funded?

For many tutors, the politics and mechanics of public funding within the learning and skills sector are opaque at best. Those tutors who progress to a middle management role within the FE sector need to gain an understanding of funding and its effects in terms of recruitment and provision of courses. For tutors whose role is predominantly a teaching one, funding mechanisms can seem to be both distant and obscure, and it only really becomes an issue when a tutor's practice is affected. So for the Pilates tutor, Alan Johnson's words may not be too reassuring. Then again, the provision of recreational or non-accredited adult education has been declining at a steady rate for many years now, so perhaps Johnson is not saying anything new. Decisions as to which kinds of course attract public subsidy and which do not will always be tinged with disagreement at best and controversy at worst. Community-based adult education courses range from learning Spanish, to buying and selling on the internet, to how to use a mobile phone. Are courses such as these more or less worthy of public funding than Pilates or plumbing?

For tutors in some curriculum areas, the fluidity of funding can be an understandable cause for concern. Typically, many tutors who are employed on part-time and temporary contracts may not know, in August, how many hours of teaching they will be doing in September. Tutors on permanent contracts may find themselves teaching different courses because those programmes that fall in their principal area of expertise have been cancelled due to lack of numbers. With courses having to be financially viable, tutors may find themselves either closing courses because the fees are prohibitive, or expanding class sizes to make the course financially worthwhile.

External agencies and organisations

In the discussion on Alan Johnson's speech, a number of stakeholders who are external to the immediate context of a college or adult education centre have been referred to. So what are these, and other, organisations, and how do they impact on education and training provision? What follows is a brief summary of the work of four important organisations: the Department for Education and Skills (DfES); the Sector Skills Development Agency (SSDA); the Quality Improvement Agency for Lifelong Learning (QIA); and the Office for Standards in Education (Ofsted).

The Department for Education and Skills

Although it is important to remember that not all education and training are funded by the government, the DfES is responsible for driving education policy. While a history of governmental approaches to education and training is beyond the scope of this book, a survey of recent activity might be useful.

When the Labour government came to power in 1997, one of the first things it did that was of importance and relevance to education and training was to publish a Green Paper called *The learning age: a renaissance for a new Britain* (a Green Paper is a government publication that sets out proposals and ideas, but does not constitute a commitment to a specific form of action or piece of legislation). According to *The learning age*, lifelong learning policy would need to be established along two lines. Firstly, for individuals, lifelong learning will help people develop the new skills that they will need to maintain their employability (and prevent themselves from being socially excluded). With 'jobs for life' being a thing of the past, and with more and more jobs requiring specific skills and qualifications, individuals would have to take part in lifelong learning so that they can change jobs or careers when necessary. Secondly, for the country as a whole, if we are to compete with other countries in the global marketplace, then our labour force needs to be flexible so that it can be redeployed quickly in response to international economic trends.

A number of government initiatives and pieces of legislation have set out to address issues such as skills gaps, low rates of adult literacy and numeracy, the relatively low take-up of further education in the UK and the comparatively low achievement of qualifications at level three in the UK, compared to Europe as a whole. The most recent government paper, *Further education: raising skills, improving life chances*, was published in 2006, two months before Alan Johnson's replacement of Ruth Kelly as Secretary of State for Education and Skills, and set out an ambitious programme for reform of the learning and skills sector, including the development of more Centres of Vocational Excellence to allow more institutions to specialise in particular areas of the curriculum, the provision of free tuition for all 19–25 year olds who have yet to achieve level three qualifications, and a new, simpler vocational qualifications framework based around a specialised diploma.

Of course, government action is not restricted to the reform of education and training as solely a concern for economic and business interests. Other recent government activity has impacted on, for example, both the professional status of tutors in the learning and skills sector (as discussed in Chapter 4) and the opportunities available for an increasingly diverse body of learners in the sector as a whole (as discussed in Chapter 9).

Sector Skills Development Agency

There are 25 Sector Skills Councils (SSCs), each representing a different area of industry or business, and which are funded and monitored by the SSDA. Representing the interests of business and industry, SSCs have a broad remit that includes addressing the skills gaps that are found in some areas of the economy, and working with other stakeholders to improve learning. SSCs play an important role in the current 14–19 curriculum reform agenda, including the creation of a new credit and qualifications framework, drawing up national occupational standards (which qualifications will need to address) and developing programmes of education and training such as foundation and advanced apprenticeships, and foundation degrees. Many tutors will be aware of the work of SSCs in their own curriculum areas. Not all tutors are aware that Lifelong Learning UK is also an SSC which, in common with other SSCs, is responsible for setting appropriate national occupational standards for all those working in post-16 education and training. In a way, LLUK sets the curriculum for teacher training for the learning and skills sector.

Quality Improvement Agency for Lifelong Learning

The QIA was established in April 2006, taking over the work previously done by the Learning and Skills Development Agency (LSDA). The prime remit of the QIA is the delivery of the government's Quality Improvement Strategy for the learning and skills sector, set out in *Further education: raising skills, improving life chances*, and which itself subsumes the earlier government strategy *Success for All*. In addition, the QIA remit includes issues such as increasing employer engagement with the learning and skills sector, improving learning and teaching, and reducing inadequate provision (as identified by Ofsted). The QIA remit ranges across the sector as a whole, and includes Skills for Life, the education and training of offenders, the professional training of subject learning coaches (as discussed in Chapter 4), the STAR awards for outstanding achievement by practitioners in the learning and skills workplace, and the carrying out and dissemination of appropriate research.

The Office for Standards in Education

Even among the very newest entrants to the learning and skills workplace, Ofsted needs little introduction. From time to time, the news that a school or college has failed an Ofsted inspection and been forced to close or be thoroughly overhauled makes its way into the public consciousness. Originally established to inspect the quality of provision in schools, Ofsted's remit was expanded in 2000 by the Learning and Skills Act. In collaboration with the Adult Learning Inspectorate (ALI), Ofsted is now responsible for the inspection of all provision in the post-compulsory sector, and also for the inspection of teacher training for the learning and skills sector. From April 2007, Ofsted and the ALI are due to merge into one inspectorate, provisionally called the Office for Standards in Education, Children's Services and Skills.

REFLECTIVE TASK

You might be more familiar with some of these organisations than others. Ofsted is a well-known feature of college life to all tutors, no matter how long they have worked there: many colleges carry out their own internal quality review processes using the Ofsted Common Inspection Framework as a template. Some of the work of the DfES may be more or less familiar: subject learning coaches occupy an increasingly high-profile position, but tutors may not necessarily stay up to date with government White Papers. SSCs or the QIA may be relatively unknown quantities.

Spend time thinking about these agencies, and any others that you have encountered in your professional life as a tutor. To what extent can you trace their influence in your working practices? Do they affect you quite directly, or hardly at all, and why do you think that is? Does it matter if you are full-time or part-time, or does the subject that you teach make a difference? If you are a full-time trainee teacher, perhaps about to go on placement, take the time to talk to your new colleagues and to your mentor about Ofsted inspections, the STAR awards, and the like. How do you think these organisations have influenced the teacher training qualification that you are currently working towards?

Watching tutors at work

There are a lot of different people and organisations with a legitimate interest in the work done by tutors: government departments, funding bodies and representatives of industry are among those stakeholders who are at one remove from the 'front line' of delivery, but are nonetheless highly influential. With so much public money at stake, and so many policy decisions at work, it is hardly surprising that external stakeholders such as these demand constant scrutiny of the sector. Audit, inspection and observation are all components of a far-reaching quality assurance process that seeks to reassure all those concerned that taxpayers' money is being well spent and that the provision that it pays for is fit for purpose. Moreover, as a greater proportion of costs is borne by the consumers of educational products – learners and those employers who sponsor them – so this reassurance of value for money becomes more widespread. Tutors, and the organisations within which they work, have become increasingly accountable for the service that they provide. And it is through a robust quality assurance process that provision can be deemed as fit for purpose, or identified as requiring intervention.

Different policies and procedures for assessing fitness for purpose are normally organised within a single, strategic approach. The management and coordination of these different evaluation activities is not left to chance; rather, different stakeholders communicate on a regular basis and all work towards an overall scheme for ensuring the quality of educational provision. Such an approach can be defined as quality assurance. Although there is no fixed definition of quality in education, the use of the word tends to imply an active concern, on the part of tutors, providers and awarding bodies, to provide the best service possible for the customers – the students. Programmes of study must be rigorous, well resourced and offer value for money. Teachers and trainers must have up-to-date qualifications and experience. The programme must be fit for the purpose for which it was intended, meeting those levels of competence or performance which have been set down by awarding bodies.

It is important to note that the learning and skills sector is far from alone in being so increasingly accountable to its customers. Over the last 30 years or so, organisations within the public sector more generally have embraced (more or less willingly) a private-sector ethos. At the time of writing this book, the continued ingress of the private sector into the National Health Service is a source of much political debate. In the learning and skills sector, the incorporation of further education colleges, some 14 years ago, represents the moment when a private-sector model was imposed on tertiary education. Within this ethos, education is not so much a right or an obligation, but a product. Learners are redefined as consumers and colleges, and community education and adult education centres compete in a free market for their custom. Providers strive for efficiency and profitability. The assumption behind this approach is that the imposition of a competitive free-market model will drive up standards of learning and teaching, producing the best possible product for the best possible price.

There is not enough space in this chapter to discuss the impact of incorporation, nor to explore the points of view of its defenders and its detractors: some of these issues will be returned to in Chapter 6, and suggestions for further reading are provided at the end of that chapter. The immediate focus, however, is on the tutor and, specifically, those aspects of the tutor's professional practice that can be seen as being influenced by the current conditions of the sector.

Tutors and the audit culture

In essence, the single biggest aspect of tutors' professional lives that can be seen as being a product of incorporation, and the growing political and industrial capital attached to the sector, is that of accountability. Or, to put it another way, tutors are no longer trusted to get on with doing their work free of monitoring and management (and the proliferation of managers within the learning and skills sector over the last 14 years is not a coincidence). Whether it is a funding body demanding value for money or an awarding body monitoring the delivery of a curriculum, the work of tutors is under constant scrutiny. So how is all this surveillance carried out?

CLOSE FOCUS CLOSE FOCUS **CLOSE** FOCUS CLOSE FOCUS **CLOSE FOCUS**

Read through the following account of preparing for a lesson observation. In this account the tutor, Chloe, raises a number of issues relating to this aspect of quality assurance. As you read, compare her situation to your own professional context. Remember, she is working in a large FE college: would her experience of observation be different if she were working in a different organisational context?

Another lesson observation! This time the whole learning area is being observed as part of the internal review. In the staffroom this morning, a colleague was saying that there was going to be an Ofsted inspection next term so the college management want a test run. At least I know which week I will be observed. And I have time to get the paperwork together. The paperwork is the thing that really gets on my nerves. I need a course file, a progress file, a teaching file, and then I need all my lesson plans on the college template even though it's not very good. It just seems such a waste of time!

I was talking to the union rep about the observations, and she was really helpful. The union is happy for them to go ahead, as long as the observer is also a qualified teacher. But I know that when I was done last time, the manager who observed me did not have her Cert Ed. I asked the rep about this, but she admitted that in this case there was little that could be done.

> *I know it's not like a real Ofsted inspection, but it's still a bit of a stress. My course manager has been flapping about chasing everyone for files because he wants to see them all before observation week and I wish he'd calm down because he's winding half of the staffroom up!*

There are a number of issues to explore here.

1. Why is there so much paperwork?

Tutors do have a lot of paperwork to complete: it is an unavoidable aspect of the job. Two or three years ago, working in FE colleges tended to be more burdensome in this regard, but adult and community education providers are catching up. At one level, paperwork is the tool of audit and quality assurance: it helps demonstrate that systems are working correctly, that the right things are being done at the right time. Paperwork helps with the running of courses, the admission of learners, and the standardisation of assessment.

This is not to say that form-filling and record-keeping are a task to be endured at best or avoided at worst. Having to maintain course files can seem like a tedious job, but if such files are kept up to date, it need not be burdensome. And other kinds of paperwork, such as records of meetings with learners, or tracking sheets that record when learners have achieved particular units in a curriculum, can be extremely useful in helping tutors to keep up with how their learners are doing. Trying to remember everything can be difficult, and if a tutor is forced to be away from work due to illness, those colleagues who are standing in will need to know how the learners are getting on.

Adult education is a little different. Unsurprisingly, accredited programmes of study tend to generate a greater degree of paperwork than non-accredited programmes. But even non-accredited programmes are now seeing the introduction of informal evaluation and assessment tools, lesson plans and course files.

Undoubtedly the amount of paperwork involved is at times excessive. But it is not automatically a problem. And while there will always be those long-serving tutors who complain about the amount of form-filling that has to be done these days, the reality is that it is an unavoidable aspect of working in the sector, and that it is far better to be reconciled to it than to be fruitlessly opposed.

2.   Who should be observing whom?

Chloe's comment that a previous observation was carried out by a manager who did not hold a Certificate in Education is relatively uncommon, but not unknown. Fento, the predecessor to LLUK, began operating in 1998 and published the standards for teaching and supporting learning in further education in England and Wales the following year. And while new staff in the sector were obliged to work towards teaching qualifications, some existing staff did slip through the net. In some areas, notably adult and community education, there was less of an impetus to gain relevant teaching qualifications. Over time, however, the assumption must be that as the workforce changes – people retire, new people enter the profession – so the percentage of practitioners with qualifications increases. And the new LLUK standards are designed to apply to the sector as a whole, whereas the Fento standards, by definition, were tailored more to the mainstream FE sector.

A situation such as this would not arise during an Ofsted inspection, but can still occur in some workplace settings. And it is an uncomfortable one. College observation and inspection policies include a complaints and appeals procedure (as does Ofsted), but it is perhaps not surprising that Chloe has not taken up the opportunity. Nor can the union help: an agreed policy of using suitably qualified observers is one thing, but if a member of staff has been in post for a sufficient period of time, it is not always possible to ask that member of staff to study for a full Cert Ed qualification if their contract does not make appropriate provision. This issue will be returned to in Chapter 5.

3. How do different people respond to an inspection or observation?

It could be argued that there is a certain amount of hysteria attached to inspection or observation. After all, if a tutor is doing his or her job properly, why shouldn't an external observer sit in? What's all the fuss about?

Of course, responses to the Ofsted regime, and to the observation process more generally, are more complex than this: the artificial nature of the inspection process can lead to a similarly artificial response from the tutor: this issue is discussed in more detail in Chapter 5. A rationale for the inspection process in itself rests within the audit culture. As part of a broad quality-assurance approach, external monitoring makes sense as a way of counteracting the subjectivity that can accompany internal quality-review processes. On the other hand, the constant need to supply this audit culture with the paperwork that it needs can lead tutors to feel that the paperwork is seen as being more important than the actual teaching that they are doing.

And there are broader issues at stake to do with the nature of professionalism: can't a professional tutor simply be trusted to do their work? This issue will be explored further in Chapter 6.

A definition of quality

For tutors, whether full- or part-time, whether working in a large college or a small community centre, quality assurance can be seen as being embedded in all aspects of professional practice. And while the procedures that surround it can sometimes be burdensome, the underpinning commitment to quality must surely be unquestioned. But if quality assurance is the process by which quality is maintained and enhanced, what is meant by 'quality'?

Perhaps unsurprisingly, notions of quality are the subject of debate. At the immediate level of learning and teaching, a tutor's definition of quality might be shaped by a number of issues, including:

- **the number of contact hours allocated for a group of learners;**
- **the number of learners in a group;**
- **the availability of resources and the quality of teaching accommodation.**

And there will always be a need to make do with facilities and situations that are less than perfect: adult education tutors, for example, tend to have to work in all manner of locations and with relatively few resources compared to tutors in a large organisation. But if equipment is lacking, class sizes are too large and an ever-growing syllabus has to be delivered over fewer teaching hours, surely quality will suffer?

For managers, the focus of quality can be somewhat different. With more of a concern for the broader financial and even political issues that impact on the learning and skills sector, a manager's definition of quality might consider different aspects, for example:

- **high retention and achievement rates;**
- **courses that are delivered within budget restrictions.;**
- **successful inspection by Ofsted or validation by an awarding body.**

This is not to say that managers systematically ignore the issues that tutors might concentrate on. But the demands of a learning and skills sector that rests on notions of a free market mean that if a course is not breaking even, irrespective of the dedication and hard work of a popular tutor, then it may have to be closed.

Class sizes as a defining factor of professionalism

Things are not always clear cut. In the previous chapter, the first case study explicitly drew attention to class sizes as a location for disagreement between the interests of tutors, who would seek to limit a class size for pedagogical reasons, and the interests of managers, who would seek to maximise a class size, within certain limits, for reasons of profitability. This is a crude distinction, perhaps, but a familiar one to tutors in college settings. But what about an adult education tutor? For a self-employed tutor who has hired a venue, prepared marketing materials and devoted time and effort to designing an evening course, a larger number of learners will bring in a greater amount of money in terms of admission fees. Does a tutor in a situation such as this seek to maximise the profitability of the evening programme, or restrict the number of learners that they allow to enrol for the sake of a pedagogical commitment?

A SUMMARY OF **KEY POINTS**

In this chapter we have looked at a number of key themes:

> The differing and, at times, conflicting interests of different stakeholders: government, funding bodies, employers, and tutors.
> The ways in which different external bodies and agencies impact on the tutor's professional practice.
> The nature of quality assurance in the learning and skills sector.

It would be nice to think that managers trust tutors to get on with their jobs, even though the level of evaluation and audit that many tutors encounter during their working lives would tell a different story. It would also be nice to think that government ministers trust tutors to get on with their work, but the proliferation of Acts of Parliament, strategies and initiatives enacted over the last 30 years or so rather belies this. To prevent tutors from feeling entirely put upon, it is worth remembering that the management and governance of colleges are also a subject for Ofsted's attention. So, if you are currently working as a tutor in a college or adult education institution, why not look up your employer's most recent Ofsted report on the internet, and see how the management scored?

FURTHER READING FURTHER READING **FURTHER READING** FURTHER READING

Journal article

This article raises a number of useful issues.

Commons, P K (2003) The contribution of inspection, self-assessment, investors in people and the inclusive learning quality initiative to improving quality in further education sector colleges: an initial exploration, *Journal of Further and Higher Education*, 27 (1), 27–46

Useful websites

The website for the Quality Assurance Agency for Lifelong Learning is: **www.qia.org.uk/**

The full text of the Alan Johnson 'plumbers not Pilates' speech can be found at: **www.qia.org.uk/aboutus/uploads/Alan_Johnson_summer_conference_speech7June2006.doc**

Information about Sector Skills Councils can be found at: **www.ssda.org.uk/default.aspx?page=2101**

The *Common inspection framework for inspecting education and training* can be found at the Ofsted website: **www.ofsted.gov.uk**

3
Codes of practice

Thinking about codes of practice

Throughout the two previous chapters, we have considered a variety of issues and themes relating to professional behaviour in the learning and skills sector. Thus far, our understanding of professional behaviour has been based on socially constructed ideas about professionalism that can be hard to pin down. Talking about these ideas from the point of view of different stakeholders in education and training can, as we have seen, lead to differences of opinion between what constitutes professional behaviour: there are lots of areas for debate – and disagreement. At the same time, there exists a clearly identifiable body of core professional values. That is to say, there are ways of behaving or acting in a teaching or training capacity that are undeniably characteristic of a 'professional' at work.

Many professions take a more active role in this debate about what constitutes professional conduct. Rather than remaining satisfied with those notions of professional behaviour that exist in society in general, many professions have sought to circumscribe the actions and behaviours of practitioners, to create some sort of mechanism by which the conduct of the members of the profession can be standardised, or regulated, or codified. Typically, this is done through a professional organisation, membership of which entails, among other things, commitment to particular and specified regulations about how work in the profession should be carried out, usually written down in a code of practice. Nor is this kind of activity new: the idea that members of particular occupations should all conform to specified standards of work can be found in the craft and trade guilds of medieval England, some 800 years ago and more.

The work of teachers, trainers and tutors in the learning and skills sector is now governed by such bodies of standards, and two key organisations are involved in this process: Lifelong Learning UK (LLUK) and the Institute for Learning (IfL). However, this was not always the case: only a decade ago, there were no agreed national standards for teachers in the sector; nor were there any standard, nationally recognised and applied requirements for professional teaching qualifications within the sector.

From Fento to LLUK

The Further Education National Training Organisation (Fento) began operating in 1998, in the same year that the government called for a more comprehensive approach to the training of teachers for the post-16 sector. The following year, Fento published the *Standards for teaching and supporting learning in further education in England and Wales*. The standards set out the skills and knowledge that were deemed essential to the role of the teacher or trainer in further education. This is not to say that before the Fento standards were published there was no training provided specifically for teachers working in further, adult or community education. What the Fento standards did provide was a national framework that could be recognised as providing a sector-wide body of standards.

From 1 January 2005 a new organisation, LLUK, began operating as the body responsible for – among other things – the professional development of all employees in the field of lifelong learning. A subsidiary organisation called Standards Verification UK took over the role of approving and endorsing teacher training qualifications in the post-compulsory sector that was once carried out by Fento, which has now ceased to exist. Additionally, the DfES published a document called *Equipping our teachers for the future: reforming initial teacher training for the learning and skills sector*. This document set out a timetable for changes to teacher training in the post-16 sector which culminated in a new range of qualifications, backed up by a new set of occupational standards which replaced the existing Fento standards in 2007.

The decision to rewrite the standards rested on two ideas. Firstly, the old Fento standards were perceived as being suitable as standards for qualified and experienced tutors, but perhaps of less value as outcomes of initial teacher training programmes. Secondly, the old standards could be seen as having focused quite closely on further education colleges, at the expense of the broader areas of practice within the learning and skills sector, such as work-based learning and community education.

The Institute for Learning

The professional interests of teachers in primary and secondary schools are represented by the General Teaching Council for England (GTC), which was established in 2000; the professional interests of teachers in higher education institutions are represented by the Higher Education Academy, formed in 2004, replacing the earlier Institute for Learning and Teaching in Higher Education, formed in 1999. With these bodies established, the learning and skills sector was alone in lacking a comparable professional organisation, prior to the formation of the IfL in 2002. The code of practice of the IfL is broadly similar to those of other, comparable professional organisations, and will be discussed in more detail below.

Codes of practice in action

The next step, therefore, is to think about codes of practice, how they work and what they do, and what kinds of things they talk about. We shall spend some time thinking about three codes of practice. Firstly, we shall look at the code of practice of the IfL. Then we shall look briefly at comparable documents from two other professional organisations that are represented in the learning and skills curriculum: the Association of Accounting Technicians (AAT) and the Register of Exercise Professionals (REPs). It is important for us to consider other such professional organisations. Many tutors in the learning and skills sector are members of more than one professional body: a tutor may be a member of both the IfL and of a body that represents their area of expertise. It is quite common for tutors to embody what is termed 'dual-professionalism', that is to say, a sense of professional commitment that derives from two sources. This issue is discussed in more detail in Chapter 6. For now, it is sufficient to note that many tutors will derive their understanding of, and commitment to, professional conduct from their subject specialism (their technical, professional or vocational background) as well as their role as a tutor.

1. The Institute for Learning

In *Equipping our teachers for the future: reforming initial teacher training for the learning and skills sector*, the role of the IfL is set out in detail, and includes QTLS registration, registration of CPD for tutors in the learning and skills sector (which is discussed in the following chapter), and liaison with the GTC and the Higher Education Academy. And there is a broader role for the IfL as well: 'we want the Institute to have an influential voice representing teachers in the sector'; 'specific tasks will include modelling good practice across the sector' (DfES, 2004, p15). These last two statements sum up nicely both the core mission of the IfL, and the core rationale of the code of professional practice, in draft form at the time of writing this book:

The Code
1. *Recognise that learners and learning are our core responsibilities, and act appropriately.*
2. *Recognise and respect the uniqueness of each individual.*
3. *Be honest, clear and open in all communications, acting with integrity and fairness, and challenging discrimination.*
4. *Contribute to the success of the college by actively seeking to develop innovative, effective and efficient ways of achieving the college's goals.*
5. *Be informed about and fulfil our legal responsibilities.*
6. *Challenge any abuse of privileged relationships, respecting and protecting confidentiality.*
7. *Ensure that our work conforms to external and internal quality standards.*
8. *Request and use resources responsibly, efficiently and effectively.*

(**www.ifl.ac.uk/members_area/code_prof.html**)

REFLECTIVE TASK

REFLECTIVE TASK

After reading through the draft code, go back through the preceding two chapters of this book. To what extent do you think that the professional standards listed here are reflected in the issues discussed before? Think about your own experiences of working as a tutor in the learning and skills sector: this might be paid employment, or on placement during a programme of teacher training. Do you think that this code adequately reflects the practice or conduct of different teachers and trainers?

In fact, this is just one part of a broader code that includes a code of ethics, and a code of good environmental practice. All of these are available from the IfL website.

2. The Association of Accounting Technicians

The AAT *Guidelines on professional ethics* make an overt link between the good standing of the profession and the need for members to maintain a professional and ethical approach, as laid out in their guidelines, which apply to both full members (that is, qualified accountants) and student members (students working towards an appropriate qualification at a further education college, for example) alike (this is also true for the IfL). While stressing that the guidelines are not meant to be rigid rules, they do set out a number of fundamental principles, which include: integrity, objectivity, professional and technical competence, due care, confidentiality, and professional behaviour. Unsurprisingly, perhaps, several of the AAT guidelines coincide with IfL guidelines, including: a requirement for professional competence through specific, accredited education and training; and the maintenance of such competence through CPD.

3. The Register of Exercise Professionals

The REPs *Code of ethical practice* similarly makes links between the establishment of a self-regulating body, a code of practice and the maintenance of the highest professional standards possible through best practice. Registration is not available to student members, however, unlike the IfL and the AAT. In this case, appropriate qualifications and competence are a prerequisite. Once again, a number of common themes emerge from the REPs code, including: a requirement for specific and up-to-date qualifications and a commitment to CPD; not to take on any task or role for which they lack appropriate qualifications; a commitment to self-evaluation and reflection; and not to condone discriminatory behaviour.

Codes of practice: a rationale

Why do professions draw up codes of practice? Why does a tutor in the learning and skills sector actually need a code of practice to work towards? Why does a member of any other profession, whether it be accountancy or exercise, need one? Four areas for consideration are offered here, although there is some overlap between these.

1. To standardise the work of the profession and guarantee a specified level of service to both users of that service and other stakeholders.

A profession's code of practice can help to standardise the working practices of its practitioners. This is particularly important if those practitioners gain access to the profession in different ways. There is no standard entry route to becoming a tutor in the learning and skills sector: people become tutors in FE colleges or adult education centres in different ways, and at different stages of life. Similarly, there are many different routes to gaining a qualification to teach in the sector: over 60 different HE institutes offer qualifications for teachers in the learning and skills sector. Through the endorsement of these qualifications, LLUK can help guarantee that they meet the needs of the sector: a qualification will only be endorsed if it covers all the different professional standards. Once qualified, tutors in the learning and skills sector commit themselves to the code of practice of the IfL. Similarly, the endorsement of accountancy qualifications by the AAT guarantees a specified level of professional knowledge and competence as appropriate to the profession of accountancy.

There is a great deal of common ground between the LLUK standards and the IfL code of practice, and this is no coincidence, given the close working relationship of the two institutions. It stands to reason that the qualifications that are required for entry to a profession map onto standards that are broadly similar to those which are adhered to by practitioners after qualification. Many professions work the same way. Indeed, one way of defining a profession at a theoretical level (and we shall return to this in more detail in Chapter 6) is through the existence of a body of qualifications that is officially endorsed by the profession in question and is necessary for all new entrants to the profession to attain.

2. To give stakeholders, and the public at large, confidence in the work of the profession and its members, and to make the work of the profession publicly accountable.

Codes of practice are invariably public documents. The members of a professional association uphold them, but anyone who might be interested can obtain a copy: the internet has made this a straightforward task. What is of interest are the reasons why making such codes publicly available has become such an accepted practice: does the public at large want or need to read the code of practice that is subscribed to by tutors in the learning and skills sector, or the code of practice of any other profession?

For the most part, of course, the answer is: 'no, they don't'. The specific details of the IfL code of practice are of little relevance to many sectors of society, of only passing relevance to some others, and of particular but nonetheless variable interest and relevance to a relative few, namely those who are stakeholders in the sector: teachers, employers, college principals, students. This is not to say that representatives of these different stakeholder groups are liable to sit down and read the IfL code in detail: it would not be unkind – or inaccurate – to suggest that, for example, many teachers will only seldom refer to the IfL code after qualifying. It is the existence of such codes, rather than paying close attention to the detail that they contain, that is important.

In the preceding chapter, we looked at the ways in which different stakeholders impact on the practices of learning and teaching in the learning and skills sector. One of the ideas discussed was that there is an expectation, in the current climate, for the work of professionals to be scrutinised and, sometimes, evaluated. The publication of codes of practice is part of this same process, a way for a professional body to declare its good practices, sound philosophies and good intentions. The very fact of having a code of practice tells the wider world that this profession wants to be seen as being accountable, transparent and open.

3. To contribute to, or codify, the accepted canons of knowledge and expertise that are required by members of the profession.

Professions are defined, in part, by the expert knowledge of the professional (an issue we shall return to in Chapter 6). The most obvious statement of professional control over expert knowledge is through the endorsement of qualifications, which we have already discussed. But it is important to note that such expertise can be found in more than one place: the specialised knowledge of a teacher in the learning and skills sector, for example, resides not only in the teacher, as he or she goes about their work, but also in the textbooks used during teacher training courses, learning and teaching resources produced by the DfES Standards Unit, the IfL code of practice, and the LLUK standards.

These different sources of expert knowledge all work in quite different ways. They do not exist in isolation, nor do they simply appear overnight. Teacher training textbooks are themselves the product of broader reading and reflection and, perhaps, the experience of the author; the Standards Unit's materials, similarly, draw on a range of earlier sources, experiences and methods. Such resources as these are deliberately designed to be used by professionals in their work. The IfL code of practice and the LLUK standards are not perhaps so immediate. A book may provide a tutor with a number of suggestions or insights concerning, for example, formative assessment: a code of practice will not do this. What a code of practice will do, however, is state the importance of selecting appropriate formative assessment methods for the benefit of a group of students (professional standards EK 1.1, EK 1.2, EP 1.1 and EP 1.2, specifically). Or, to put it another way, the importance of an understanding of formative assessment principles and practice is shown, through its presence in both books and a code of practice, to be an established aspect of the specialist expertise of the professional tutor.

4. To contribute to, or codify, the accepted ethical and values-driven practices of the members of the profession.

As we have seen in the preceding two chapters, being a professional is all about an attitude, a perspective, a commitment to certain values and ethical considerations that might be related to, for example, widening participation, or a broader commitment to wanting to help your students to succeed. Some such issues are unproblematic: a commitment to challenge and not to condone any kind of discriminatory behaviour, which can be found in the REPs code of ethical practice as well as in the IfL code and the LLUK standards, is surely uncontroversial. Similarly, a commitment to confidentiality between professionals and clients (and this might be between tutors and students or between fitness instructors and clients) can also be accepted without question.

Other issues can be more complex, however, and difficult to unpack. LLUK professional value AS 4, for example, states that teachers with QTLS value 'the potential for learning to benefit people emotionally, intellectually, socially and economically, and to contribute to community sustainability'. And there is little to argue about here: it goes without saying that, having chosen to work as teachers or trainers, we have some kind of commitment to the learning of our students and the benefits that accrue from participation in education and training. Once we start to unpack such statements, however, we can find some difficult issues and questions.

CASE STUDY CASE STUDY CASE STUDY CASE STUDY CASE STUDY CASE STUDY

CASE STUDY

Unpacking codes of practice

Assigning intellectual or economic benefits to learning seems to make sense. It stands to reason that learning, in some way, is good for us at an intellectual level, in the same way that doing Sudoku puzzles is said to be good exercise for the brain. Similarly, the economic benefits are obvious: the right qualifications can help people to change jobs or careers. Emotional benefits can also be seen as a consequence of learning: teacher training courses and books are full of discussions about the impact of learning on motivation and confidence, and a lack of these is often cited as a barrier to participation in learning.

Let us focus on the last of these three issues: in fact, there is significant scope for debate. Simply assuming that learning leads to emotional benefits leaves all kinds of assumptions unchallenged. Is it a good thing that teaching and learning processes should focus on emotional issues, on the affective domain? Is empathy a desirable quality for a tutor to possess? Is the role of the tutor to stretch and challenge the student or to enhance their self-esteem, and are these compatible or incompatible aims?

REFLECTIVE TASK
REFLECTIVE TASK

In the following piece of reflective writing, Robin explores a critical incident that arose from a feedback session with one of his students. As you read, consider Robin's reaction to what happened, and think about how you might react in a similar situation.

Feedback tutorials today, and I had to give Sue her work back again – simply of too poor a standard for even a bare pass, despite the lengthy feedback session that we had after her first submission. I'm not even sure that she should be doing this course, but she was quite adamant at the start of term that she wanted to take it and would do the work. But she hasn't. Giving the work back isn't a big deal, though – it's all the histrionics that go with it that I find hard to deal with. Sue started crying after a few minutes and it took ages for me to calm her down and try to sort out some sort of action plan for her and what should have been a thirty minute tutorial turned into most of the afternoon – so much for catching up on my marking.

I found all this exhausting. Dealing with this is not what I am here for: I can't pass a poor piece of work just because a student is going to get upset. But neither can I do anything other than be honest in my feedback. I like to think that I'm tactful and choose my words carefully, but if a piece of work has to go back, then there's not much you can do. If I had the control over admissions that I should have, then this might not have happened, but there you go. As it is, I have had to spend hours calming her down and telling her that with the new action plan, she'll be fine. But she won't be fine – I doubt that she has what it takes for this course.

I felt quite unsettled when I got back to the staffroom. My job is to do what's best for the students, but I am a teacher and not a social worker. I know that some students are a lot less confident than others, but it shouldn't be down to me to pick them up. How am I supposed to give feedback if my students are just going to start crying if I tell them things they don't want to hear?

There are two key issues here: one can be discussed quite briefly, which is admissions to the course. Robin clearly feels that he should have more say over who comes on to the course. This is difficult, as there are significant financial issues to consider, as we discussed in Chapter 1. The second issue relates to Robin's attitude towards this particular tutor–student relationship. Robin is quite adamant that 'dealing with this is not what I am here for'. What is he referring to here? It is not the feedback process as such that is the problem, it is the emotional aspect of the encounter: the student who has burst into tears. Robin may simply be uncomfortable with dealing with a student who is upset, but there is a deeper issue to consider: to what extent is the emotional or affective domain a part of his professional role? Or, to put it another way, is his job to teach people things, or to make them feel better about themselves?

Theory focus

In an article published in 2005, Kathryn Ecclestone, Dennis Hayes and Frank Furedi tackled the issues of student self-esteem and well-being from the perspective of the professional role of the tutor. They argued that the growing focus on dealing with the emotional or self-esteem needs of students changed the working relationship between tutor and student in a number of ways:

> The closer that professionals have to move towards the expressed or attributed emotional needs of students, the harder it becomes to offer pedagogic and assessment activities that are challenging or perhaps necessarily threatening ...
>
> Teachers will have to become more emotionally open because students come to expect it or because focusing on emotional well-being overcomes disaffection from the curriculum and educational experiences on offer. In this respect, emotional well-being is an easier educational goal than developing skills and knowledge.

(Ecclestone et al, 2005, p194)

This is a powerful argument, and challenges many established ideas relating to inclusion and widening participation, both of which are central to the ethical standpoints of LLUK and IfL. We shall return to this argument in Chapter 9.

This is interesting stuff, but how is all this connected to our case study, to Robin, his tearful student, and to professional value AS 4? Quite simply, this case study is intended to demonstrate the complexity that underpins many of the different statements that codes of practice contain. To say that learning should promote emotional benefits seems right at a surface level: many tutors agree that learning enhances self-esteem and confidence. And that's fine. But are these the primary reason why tutors do what they do, or why opportunities for participation in formal education and training should be provided for all those who wish to access them? At the very least, don't professionals need some kind of licence to debate such ideas?

Things to be cautious about

Every time that anyone tries to reduce a number of ideas, issues or themes to a list that is going to be printed, distributed and read by lots of different people in different places, compromises will have to be made. When discussing the documentation that is sent out by awarding or examining bodies, for example, I have heard tutors say that the outcomes that awarding bodies set can sometimes be too general or simplistic. Similarly, the clauses of a code of practice may sometimes be too general. Then again, if they were lengthy, detailed and full of analysis and argument, they would be far too unwieldy for use. Codes of practice are not meant to be definitive statements of truth, nor are they meant to be rigid and unyielding. Nonetheless, there are some things that are worth bearing in mind when working with codes of practice.

1. They can gloss over complex issues and themes.

As seen in the case study, uncovering a fairly short and simple statement can sometimes lead to long and complex arguments about what the statement implies. This may or may not be a bad thing: on the one hand, our case study demonstrates that there is much more to say and think about relating to the emotional support that a tutor provides for a student. On the other hand, saying that a tutor needs to be supportive and friendly need not lead to controversy. There have to be a time and place for both. In the day-to-day working life of a tutor in an adult education centre or a further education college, there is often little time or space for a detailed exploration of the nature of the emotional or affective support that a tutor might be expected to provide. This is fair enough, but the possibility of debate, and even disagreement, must not be forgotten.

2. They privilege some ideas, concepts and ways of working at the expense of others.

Following on from the first point, and knowing what we know about the role of professional codes of practice in circumscribing the expert knowledge of a profession, it shouldn't come as a surprise that codes of practice privilege some ideas and ignore others. A code of practice is hardly likely to contain a list of issues or theories that are in opposition to the work or ideals of the professional body in question. So it is important to remember that there may be more to being a professional than what is found in a code of practice, and that what is to be found in a code of practice may not fit everyone's ideas about what being a professional entails. For example, the IfL code requires practitioners to 'ensure that our work conforms to external and internal quality standards'. But who gets to define 'quality'? Ofsted inspections are one of the most visible of quality assurance procedures in the learning and skills sector, and are a source of anxiety and argument for many tutors. In the previous two chapters we have alluded to the fact that managers' ideas about the professional conduct of tutors are not always in sympathy with those of the tutors themselves: the amount of paperwork and bureaucracy involved in the working life of the tutor is a good example of this.

At the same time, it is important not to treat codes of practice unfairly, or to expect them to do things that they are not intended to do. A code of practice is not a manifesto or a list of issues for a public disputation. It is a reflection of what is deemed to be best practice at the time of its creation.

3. They can be ignored or misinterpreted.

Representatives of a professional body cannot be everywhere at once. How can a professional body ensure that its members are behaving correctly, according to sound professional principles? The short answer is: they can't. But there are ways of trying to ensure this, and having a code of practice is one of them (enshrining the values of the profession in a period of education or training is another). A code of practice is written down, available on paper or online. As such, it can travel, and be picked up and read by both members and non-members of the association irrespective of where they actually live and work. What is more problematic, however, is in controlling what happens to the code of practice after that: I have made use of two codes of practice in this chapter without any kind of official sanction from the bodies involved. As for those practitioners who are members of the bodies in question, how do those bodies know that members have read the code of practice and understood it correctly? Are members really expected to read the codes of practice from cover to cover?

Codes of practice: so what do they do?

It's perfectly feasible for a practitioner to belong to a professional association, which assumes an acceptance of that association's code of practice, without ever actually reading the code of practice in question. And it's perfectly feasible for someone who is entirely unconnected to a professional body to read that body's code of practice. It hardly seems realistic, therefore, to describe a code of practice as something that by and of itself controls and orders the work of professionals.

Codes of practice need to be understood in context. They represent a simplified, 'boiled down' version of a much broader body of ideas and expectations about what a professional does, from the point of view of a specific professional association. That is to say, they sum up what that professional association thinks the members of the association should work towards or embody in their everyday working lives. Of course, these professional associations do not exist in isolation: they live in the same world as the rest of us, and are influenced, in part, by the same broader, social debates as we are – the debates and issues that we have covered in the preceding two chapters. In addition, they are influenced, more or less overtly, by the theoretical traditions that surround notions of professionalism, as we shall see in Chapter 6. A code of practice is a statement of what a professional association thinks is important, but cannot be seen as a definitive or final statement about what 'professionalism' actually is. It might get read from cover to cover; it might get ignored completely. But the fact that it is actually there is what is important: it shows us that a professional association, as one group of stakeholders in education and training, takes its responsibilities, and the responsibilities of its members, seriously.

A SUMMARY OF **KEY POINTS**

During this chapter we have looked at the following key points:

> The context for the establishment of codes of professional practice for tutors in the learning and skills sector.

> Common themes between different codes of practice that are to be found represented in the learning and skills sector.

> A rationale for codes of practice.

> The complex dilemmas and issues that can sometimes be masked by codes of practice, and how an exploration of these issues is still compatible with a commitment to professional conduct.

Professional associations in all walks of life are coming under increasing pressure to be open and transparent in their work, to be accountable, and to be seen to be so. In Chapter 6, we shall discuss this change in the nature of professionalism, and explore the reasons why professionals are more open about their work than was the case a generation ago. For now, it is sufficient to note that this transparency is the norm, and that the promulgation of codes of practice is a part of this process.

Websites

The website for the IfL is at **www.ifl.ac.uk** The website for the Association of Accounting Technicians is at **www.aat.org.uk** The website for the Register of Exercise Professionals is at **www.exerciseregister.org** The codes of practice referred to in this chapter can all be found at the website of the relevant professional body.

Journals

This article, referred to below, is not an easy read. But it is both challenging and rewarding and definitely worth persevering with.

Ecclestone, K, Hayes, D and Furedi, F (2005) Knowing me, knowing you: the rise of therapeutic professionalism in the education of adults, *Studies in the Education of Adults*, 37 (2), 182–200

4
Continuing professional development

By the end of this chapter you should:

- have explored the place of continuing professional development (CPD) in the lives and careers of teachers and trainers in the learning and skills sector;
- considered some of the reasons why CPD is important and looked at a range of different activities that can contribute to the process;
- be aware of the activities of two organisations that have an important and expanding role to play in connection with CPD: the Institute for Learning and the DfES Standards Unit.

Professional Standards

This chapter relates to the following Professional Standards:

Professional Values:

AS 4 Reflection and evaluation of their own practice and their continuing professional development as teachers.

Professional Knowledge and Understanding:

AK 4.3 Ways to reflect, evaluate and use research to develop own practice, and to share good practice with others.

Professional Practice:

AP 4.3 Share good practice with others and engage in continuing professional development through reflection, evaluation and the appropriate use of research.

REFLECTIVE TASK

Think about the occupational or technical area in which you currently teach or train, either in employment or on placement, or within which you hope to work in the future. This might be IT, or mechanical engineering, childcare or psychology. Think of all the changes that have taken place in your specialism over the last five or ten years. What kind of impact have these changes had in terms of teaching and training within that specialism?

The role of CPD

The further education sector is diverse and fluid, with a wide variety of subjects offered to students from all kinds of backgrounds. What actually gets taught, the courses and the content, is similarly varied. Teachers and trainers often find themselves taking on additional responsibilities in terms of what they are required to teach. They might need to gain new knowledge in order to teach a new course, or they might need to gain new skills because the curriculum of an existing course has changed. Teachers cannot stand still once they have finished their teacher training courses. In fact, teacher training is very often just the beginning of a much longer process of activity and study that will continue in the workplace – in colleges, outreach centres and community education centres.

At first glance, the term 'continuing professional development' would appear quite self-explanatory. As teachers, we need to develop our skills and knowledge and understanding of our subject, our students and the colleges within which we work, throughout our working lives. And it helps us, as professionals, to be more professional. With a little more thought, however, some questions and concerns spring to mind: not everyone has the same idea of what 'being professional' means. As has been already discussed in Chapters 1 and 2, teachers, college principals and parents may have very different ideas of what being a professional actually involves. And the idea that such development is a 'continuing' process is also open to investigation. Teachers in FE colleges have busy working lives, and there may be barely time enough to prepare lessons, assess students' portfolios and deliver classes without attending training courses as well. Having spent many years working in industry and acquiring a battery of industry qualifications, and then having studied part-time for a Certificate in Education, surely now it is possible for a teacher to relax and take things a bit easy?

CPD is, in fact, an important aspect of the FE teacher's professional life. It can take many forms and have many purposes. Just as there are different notions of 'professionalism', so there are different notions of what CPD consists of, how it should be carried out, and how it should be prepared for and justified. Some activities easily lend themselves to being defined as continuing professional development: going on a training course in order to learn new teaching techniques, for example. Other activities are a little less clear-cut: is reading (to take one example) a form of CPD, or simply something that tutors should be doing anyway? Do activities organised by official institutions always count as CPD? Do activities carried out on an unofficial basis count as CPD? Who gets to 'set' the CPD 'curriculum'?

A rationale for CPD: the teacher

For the teacher or trainer, therefore, there are a number of reasons why CPD is important:

1. To update subject-specialist knowledge

In the reflective focus at the start of this chapter, attention was drawn to the fact that subject specialisms do not stand still. The things that are taught and learned change, perhaps because of new technologies, or because of new ways of looking at older ideas, or because of changing attitudes. Within different subject areas, what needs to be known and understood about that subject can and does change frequently. Motor vehicle tutors need to know about new industry standards. Beauty therapy tutors need to know about new treatments or new products that are coming into the marketplace. Students expect their tutors to be experts, and maintaining this expertise is one part of the CPD process.

2. To take account of changes to the curriculum

New technological advances or industrial standards invariably have an impact on the courses that are offered within the learning and skills sector. Many examination boards and awarding bodies work closely with trade and industry bodies in order to ensure that the curriculum is up to date and meets the needs of employers' organisations. Curriculum documents are revised or even rewritten regularly: sometimes a course will be changed from one year to the next, often with little notice. Tutors and assessors need to keep abreast of these changes to the programmes that we are involved in, in addition to acquiring the new skills and knowledge that have driven these changes.

3. To update organisational and procedural knowledge

Changes to the curriculum don't just affect the content of our lessons, however. They may lead to changes in assessment procedures, or changes in the way that the course is run in the college or the workplace as a whole. Teachers may find themselves working with different colleagues, or taking on different responsibilities within their subject team, such as second-marking students' assignments. CPD can involve learning about and taking on new workplace procedures as well as learning new subject knowledge.

4. To enhance employment prospects

It is quite common for a teacher to want to change jobs during the course of their career. Some FE teachers look to take on management responsibilities, sometimes in addition to maintaining a teaching role. Some teachers start out on a part-time basis and then decide to look for a full-time position. Trainers and assessors working in industrial or commercial settings may decide to move to work in a college, and vice versa. In these, and other, circumstances, a strong CPD record can be a real asset when making applications and attending interviews. Colleges, as employers, have their own reasons for encouraging CPD (and this will be discussed below) and will seek to employ new members of staff who can demonstrate past achievement and future potential in this regard.

5. To take account of technological changes

Changes in technology can have an impact on our teaching practice that goes beyond the confines of the subject specialism: we do not need to be teachers of a computing course to gain benefits from using technology in our workplaces. This can relate directly to teaching, for example in the use of interactive whiteboards in the classroom; or it may relate to course administration, such as using a computer to store student records.

6. To take account of legislative changes

Sometimes, the duties carried out by teachers change not because of changes to the course or to the subject matter, but due to broader changes in the world in which we live. The impact of the Disability Discrimination Act on FE colleges is a good example. According to the Act, discrimination against a student may come about in two ways: firstly, by failing to make 'reasonable adjustment' for a student with a disability; secondly, by treating a student with a disability 'less favourably' for a reason related to that disability. Of course, colleges as institutions have a responsibility to prevent discrimination, but that does not mean that individual teachers should assume that the college would take care of everything. After all, it is often the individual teacher who is the first point of contact with the student.

7. To maintain a licence to practise

Many professionals, such as first aid trainers, solicitors and social workers, are in fact obliged to take part in a certain amount of CPD each year. These CPD activities are measured in terms of time spent engaged with them, and are offered by approved providers. Planned reforms for the initial training of teachers in the learning and skills sector include the obligation for teachers to take part in annual CPD. According to *Equipping our teachers for the future,* which was published by the DfES in 2004: 'each teacher will need to renew their licence on a regular basis by completing an annual tariff of appropriate continuing professional development (CPD)' (p8). This licence to practise, and the monitoring of CPD that it requires, will (it is assumed) be administered by the Institute for Learning (IfL).

Further education: raising skills, improving life chances was published by the DfES in 2006, and set out a mandatory framework for CPD for FE teachers for the first time: 'all teaching practitioners to fulfil, at the very least, 30 hours of CPD a year, with a reduced amount for part time teachers' (p51). This paper also provides one answer to the question posed at the start of this chapter: who gets to 'set' the CPD 'curriculum'? It goes without saying that the DfES would be interested in influencing CPD, and the paper goes on to say that teachers will have to 'maintain a portfolio of CPD that shows evidence of industrial/subject updating, including membership of appropriate professional bodies, development of skills in subject teaching, including the effective application of e-learning techniques, application of diversity and equal opportunity principles, and use of learner feedback to improve performance' (p52).

8. To stay fresh and involved

Finally, it is worth remembering that staying involved and engaged with new ways of teaching and learning in different subject specialisms can keep teachers fresh, creative and inspiring. It is not difficult for students to spot those teachers who are tired and jaded, and lack enthusiasm for the subject that they teach. This is not to say that from time to time a teacher cannot be allowed an off-colour day at work. But enthusiasm is infectious, and those teachers who show that they enjoy their subject, not least by seeking to stay fresh and up to date, can pass this enthusiasm on to their students more effectively than those teachers who are going through the motions.

A rationale for CPD: the college

Colleges, as employers as well as providers of learning, also have reasons for wanting to encourage CPD within the workforce – the teachers. Some of these coincide to some degree with the teachers' rationales that have just been discussed.

1. To improve the student experience

As mentioned above, students have all kinds of expectations about their teacher. Fluent expertise in their subject area is just one of these. Others include punctuality in marking and returning assignments, an understanding of college procedures (ranging from where the student ID cards are issued to where accessibility equipment for a student with a disability can be obtained), or even simply a sympathetic ear when things – not necessarily just studies – are not going well.

2. To maximise the effectiveness of staff

Employers often provide or encourage appropriate CPD activities to address those students' needs, which can at the same time help the teachers expand their professional knowledge. This might be procedural: for example, organising learning support for students with disabilities; or related to teaching and learning, for example, the college may use lesson observations to highlight areas for improvement in the classroom (this last issue in particular is controversial, and will be discussed in more detail below). At the same time, colleges are aware of the changing needs of the curriculum and of any employers with whom they work, and will make time for CPD that allows staff to stay up to date in their subject.

3. To improve the staff experience

Although it may come as a surprise to some, the majority of colleges do endeavour to provide a positive and worthwhile work environment for their staff. It makes sense for colleges to do so. Just as new staff need supporting in their first weeks and months as teachers, so existing staff need supporting in enhancing and expanding their professional roles. By giving staff the opportunity to develop their practice, colleges can also foster the sense that staff feel valued by their employer.

4. To improve accountability

Providers of education and training are accountable to a variety of stakeholders: boards of governors, parents, students, funding bodies, government agencies, fee sponsors and employers. The work that colleges do can be scrutinised by these stakeholders quite easily: Ofsted (the Office for Standards in Education) reports, for example, are freely available for downloading from the internet. One of the areas in which the performance or effectiveness of a college is measured is the quality of the teaching provided: in other words, how good are the teachers at their job? In this regard, CPD is important for colleges in helping to ensure that the teaching staff are working as well as they possibly can.

PRACTICAL TASK PRACTICAL TASK **PRACTICAL TASK** PRACTICAL TASK **PRACTICAL TASK**

Formal CPD policies and procedures exist throughout the further education sector. Where can guidelines about CPD be found within the college in which you work or in which you are undertaking, or have already undertaken, a teaching placement? What kinds of CPD activities are encouraged or offered within your college, and why? And who decides which CPD activities are appropriate for different teachers?

Planning and preparing for CPD

Having established that CPD is good for both employers and employees, the next questions are: how and when do we decide on a particular CPD activity? Who identifies which teacher would like or would need a specific training or development opportunity? Is the choice of CPD activity always down to the individual teacher?

At some point, someone is going to have to make a decision about professional development and training. The exact mechanics of this process vary between different institutions, however. In this first extract from his journal, David, who is a newly qualified teacher in a further education college, reflects on his recent teacher training, his first year as a teacher, and on the next stage of his professional development.

One of the things that has surprised me is how much more there is to learn. By the time I had finished my teacher training, I was ready to give studying a rest and just get down to work. During my first year of teaching after finishing my Cert Ed, there have been two things that have really stood out. One was the help that I got from everyone else in the staffroom, getting to know how the college worked and things like that. The other was how much more stuff there was to learn that I thought could have been part of the Cert Ed, but I guess there isn't time to fit everything in. Next year, the college is going to have a larger cohort of 14–16 year old learners and I am going to be tutoring a group of them. This year I have taught 17- and 18-year olds, just like I did during my placement. And I was really worried at first about teaching younger groups. But Jayne and I talked about this at my appraisal meeting, and she was really helpful. She'd found a training course being run in September – a whole-day course all about working with a 14–16 group, looking at managing behaviour, dealing with disruption, all those things I wasn't really used to.

CLOSE FOCUS CLOSE FOCUS **CLOSE FOCUS** CLOSE FOCUS **CLOSE FOCUS**

Before reading on, take time to note down the issues raised by David's journal entry. How has his decision to go on a training course been arrived at? Why is this training course a good idea for David at this time? What does the extract tell you about the organisation's attitude to David's professional development?

The college is increasing the number of 14–16 year old students who will be attending courses next year: this is a reflection of a broader shift in provision in the FE sector that has been under way in recent years. It is recognised that teaching the 14–16 group will be very different for David – or, indeed, for any tutor – compared to teaching the 'traditional' 16–19 age group or adult learners. Having found an appropriate training programme, Jayne has organised college funding for David to attend the event. This is an excellent example of staff development meeting the needs of both the teacher and the institution.

In this second journal extract, Kim, who is a numeracy teacher with several years' experience, describes a very different CPD event.

Yesterday was the staff training day. The whole of the basic skills team had to meet in our base room, and then we were going to go to the resource centre to see some new stuff on the college network, and we would be there until lunch. The college has decided to move onto a whole new computer-based assessment package for literacy and numeracy, and all the diagnostic testing is going to be done online. It's great – the marks are all collated by the computer program so that I get a clear breakdown of how everybody did. When the students get their results, the program highlights which bits they did well in and which bits they need to practise. So we all sat down and did both the literacy and the numeracy tests.

I enjoyed it. I'm quite happy using a PC anyway, but I can see how for some of us it will have been good practice. The best thing about it was that when my students are taking these tests at the start of the next course, I can help them if they get stuck with the PC from a technical point of view.

What are the issues relating to CPD that are raised by Kim's diary entry? What is the context for the CPD that she describes, and how will it enhance or improve her professional practice?

Cross-college training days, such as that described by Kim, are often found within the FE sector as a whole. It is common practice for several such training days to be held during the course of the academic year, when subject or curriculum teams take part in joint CPD activities. It is important for Kim and her colleagues to get to know the package before use, so that she can more reliably help and guide students through the process, and so that she knows how and in what manner the results are produced and collated. Kim is a confident information and learning technologies (ILT) user, but she acknowledges in her journal the fact that for some of her colleagues, this training will have been good practice in ILT use generally, as well as practice in the computer-based assessment specifically. In this example, the college's institution-wide decision to move to this computer-based assessment of the numeracy and literacy needs of students has necessitated appropriate staff training. At the same time, it is a worthwhile CPD experience for Kim, who has had an opportunity to enhance her knowledge and skills of the use of ILT within an education and training context.

In this third and final journal extract, Wendy, a business studies lecturer, describes a recent lesson observation carried out by her line manager, Chris, and the feedback received from it.

The lesson observation: this was not in itself a cause of worry for me. I had become accustomed to lesson observations during my teacher training, and we have college observations every year, so I am in fact quite used to having an observer present in any given session. I had told the group that the lesson would be observed, and they were fine. In fact, I am sure that the students are as used to it as we are.

The feedback session: Chris began by thanking me for helping the process go so smoothly, before moving to discuss the observation in detail. These college observations are quite different from the teacher training ones, on reflection. The college observations are modelled very closely on Ofsted inspections – I assume this is as a form of practice, to allow us all to become accustomed to the process well in advance of a proper inspection. Being given a grade is quite a daunting experience. Nonetheless, it was helpful. Some useful points were raised: the design of one of the handouts could have been clearer, I agree, and the small group exercise did not go quite according to plan. On balance, I agree that the instructions I gave were a little muddled. I don't agree that I should have done less talking at the start, however: many of the students need a more formal introduction to new topics, and while there is a time and place for being student-centred, there is also a time and place for a tutor-led approach. But Chris raised some good and helpful points, and has given me some things to consider.

REFLECTIVE TASK
REFLECTIVE TASK

Before reading on, spend a few moments considering those occasions when you have been observed while delivering a session. This observation may have been part of a teacher training programme, or a college-based observation programme, or even an Ofsted or ALI (Adult Learning Inspectorate) observation.

> In what ways did these observations help you as a teacher in developing and reflecting on your own practice?

Observations of teaching practice as part of a college-based appraisal system, such as that described by Wendy, are a common feature of life in the further education. At one level, her analysis is spot-on: at one level, they are simply rehearsals for external inspections carried out by Ofsted. But they serve another purpose. By having an observer present in her classroom, Wendy gains another perspective on her teaching practice, and Chris provides another perspective, pinpointing issues for development that Wendy herself may not always notice.

RESEARCH FOCUS RESEARCH FOCUS **RESEARCH FOCUS** RESEARCH FOCUS **RESEARCH FOCUS**

Observation generally consists of a four-stage process (initial discussion, the observation itself, a follow-up discussion meeting and production of a written record). Such activities add hours to the working day. However, as NATFHE comments, without resources to expedite the process (e.g. training observers, making time available for preparation and feedback) and to support any identified development needs, the process becomes meaningless.

(Shortland, 2004, p221)

Sue Shortland is talking about higher education here, but these issues nicely sum up the concerns facing the observation processes within the further education sector as well. As with every other aspect of CPD, time is often the resource that is lacking. And without sufficient time, lesson observations run the risk of becoming mechanical processes whereby the observation is followed by a perfunctory conversation and paperwork-completion exercise, allowing little time for meaningful discussion of the observed session itself, let alone providing time to reflect on what went well in the session, and what might need development.

Identifying CPD needs

There are several procedures by which the CPD needs of teachers or trainers might be identified, therefore:

- following a staff appraisal meeting;
- following a lesson observation;
- in response to a new college-wide change of procedure;
- following changes to the curriculum (course content and/or student constituency);
- as part of an established, regular college-wide CPD policy;
- as a personal choice on the part of a member of staff (who may, for example, wish to undertake study at a higher level, or in a new subject area, or who may wish to do some research).

CPD activities and strategies

The final question is: what kinds of activities actually constitute CPD? Some have been touched on already, and what follows is by no means an exhaustive list. At the same time, not all forms of CPD are attractive to or suitable for all teachers and trainers within FE: bearing in mind the diverse nature of the FE workforce, it is unsurprising that CPD activities are similarly diverse.

1. Training days or other events offered within colleges

As can be seen from the case studies that we have already looked at, such training can be found in a variety of formats. Cross-college training days are quite common, as is the provision of other training on a less large-scale basis, during the academic year as a whole. In many colleges, staff development officers often organise training events that are run by members of college staff for the benefit of other colleagues (for example, in learning how to use a new computer program, or becoming acquainted with new methods of ensuring accessibility to learning for students with disabilities).

2. Attending external courses and other external training and development events

Throughout the academic year, it is quite common to find external training and development events run by a variety of organisations. Private training companies run workshops for teachers such as 'Dealing with disaffected students'. Sometimes, colleges will buy in such training; at other times, they will encourage staff to attend, or agree to a teacher's suggestion that attendance would be beneficial. Awarding or examining bodies often run training days for a number of reasons. A training event might be delivered to introduce colleges and teachers to fundamental changes to a syllabus, or to ensure that marking and assessment procedures are standardised across colleges.

3. Returning to study

This is perhaps the most obvious form of CPD, but none the less valuable for that. Enrolling on a course leading to higher professional, technical or vocational qualifications can be highly satisfying, and may sometimes attract financial support from an employer. The significant drawback to such study is the time involved, however. As in-service trainee FE teachers know only too well, it can be very difficult to balance work, family and study commitments.

4. Attending conferences

Attending conferences is quite common among practitioners working in higher education. Within the FE sector it is less common, which is perhaps regrettable. Nevertheless, organisations such as the LSDA (Learning and Skills Development Agency) and journals such as the *Journal of Vocational Education and Training* hold regular conferences that attract FE as well as HE practitioners.

5. Mentoring

Mentoring strategies within the FE sector are highly variable. While many colleges run formal induction activities for new members of staff, longer-term mentoring of new colleagues can be time-consuming, difficult to organise and expensive. A number of pilot schemes have been completed recently that have sought to explore the difficulties of providing a universal mentoring scheme for FE. Mentoring is another area earmarked for reform in *Equipping our teachers for the future*: '... mentoring of teachers in the workplace: an essential aim of the training is that teachers should have the skills of teaching in their own specialist or curriculum area ... Mentoring, either by line managers, subject experts or experienced teachers in related curriculum areas, is essential' (p8).

While mentoring can be time-consuming, it can also be highly rewarding. Discussing aspects of work with a new colleague can often lead the more experienced mentor to look again at his or her own professional practice and values.

6. Taking part in teaching observations

The example given above, drawn from Wendy's journal, of an observation carried out by a line manager, is not the only kind of observation that is encouraged by the quality-assurance procedures within colleges. Peer observations, where one teacher observes another, are also quite common. Within some teacher training programmes, it is common practice for the trainee to ask to observe an experienced colleague.

7. College appraisal meetings and reports

As part of their broader quality-assurance systems, it is now common practice for colleges to compile self-assessment reports on an annual basis. This college-wide process of evaluation is normally used to identify current areas of good practice, and also areas that require improvement. Identifying the training needs of teaching staff can form a part of the recommendations made within such reports for the next academic year.

8. Becoming a subject learning coach

Subject learning coaches work within an organisation, or between organisations, to improve teaching and learning within a particular subject area. Through sharing good practice, coaching and supporting teaching and training staff, subject learning coaches work within the framework for improving teaching and learning set out by the DfES Standards Unit. These are discussed in more detail below. When working as a subject learning coach, teachers have the opportunity to help plan the CPD of others, as well as the chance to expand their own professional role and work towards professional coaching or mentoring qualifications.

9. Reflecting on one's own teaching practice: self-evaluation

While there are disagreements over the benefits – or otherwise – of reflective practice (these arguments are rehearsed in Chapter 7), the opportunity to sit back and mull over a day's work can be, for many teachers in FE, the best opportunity to evaluate teaching practice and consider how anything – if at all – could or should have been done differently. Sometimes, this is best done in isolation. Other tutors take the opportunity to talk through dilemmas and concerns with colleagues. It isn't always easy to find time for this, but it can be a valuable activity.

In this final journal extract in this chapter, Jon, a new FE teacher, recounts a conversation that he had with his line manager, Neil.

> *So I had got back for seeing this student who hadn't handed any work in, and kept missing our tutorials. And of course once the conversation between us started, it turned out that she was having all kinds of problems with the course, and didn't really understand it, and was having a very hard time making sense of the assignments, and all the rest. At one point she was in tears. It was pretty upsetting, really, and I felt awful afterwards, even though we managed to stay friends and*

work out a way to get out of this position. I got back to the staffroom, and it was already after five, and I started talking to Neil about it and before I knew anything, it was a few minutes before six. Now, Neil didn't start saying 'oh, you could have done that differently' or anything – not judgemental at all. He just listened while I talked it out, and that was what I needed. I had done the best I could. I wasn't to know the extent of the student's problems until she and I could have a proper conversation, and Neil was a great sounding board. It's just a shame that there isn't more time for talking like that.

CPD and the part-time tutor

Regrettably, part-time tutors often miss out on some of the CPD opportunities that are available to full-time staff, or those staff who are on substantial fractional contracts (who, for example, work four days each week). For those tutors on hourly-paid contracts, the time that would be spent attending training events at their place of work is invariably unpaid. CPD events are often targeted at full-time staff, and part-time tutors can be left out of the process. Unfortunately, there is no simple remedy for this. Some colleges are very good at including part-time staff in the full range of training activities offered: others are less conscientious. Nonetheless, exploring the CPD opportunities for part-time staff in the workplace is always a worthwhile activity.

CPD and the Institute for Learning

In the previous chapter, we looked at the growing role of the Institute for Learning and its role in drawing up a code of conduct for the FE sector. Another important part of the IfL's work is in formulating a sector-wide series of policies and procedures relating to CPD. As the IfL say on their website:

> *Most other professional bodies have been asking for evidence of continuing professional development as a basic requirement of their members for many years now The IfL exists to be representative of a group of professionals who have long been undervalued. To present the strongest voice possible we must be seen to be representing a sector that is maintaining its own voluntary high standards in delivering the skills that enhance and improve the quality of learners' experiences. This is why we ask our members to be able to demonstrate that they remain in 'good professional standing' by engaging in CPD activities, throughout the lifetime of their membership.*

(www.ifl.ac.uk/cpd_portal/cpdcd/index.html)

This is very much a developmental process, and members of the IfL (and membership is open to trainee teachers as well as qualified practitioners) are encouraged to take part in a pilot programme to evaluate ways of recording and monitoring CPD activities.

CPD and the Standards Unit

As part of the *Success for all* strategy, the DfES has established the Standards Unit, which was set up in January 2003. It is responsible for – among other things – the creation and dissemination of resources for a number of different curriculum areas within the learning and skills sector, to improve the quality of teaching and learning within those areas. These resources (which include audio and video resources, games, role-play activities and written materials) are available for a number of different subject areas, including: business, entry to employment (E2E), health and social care, and land-based studies.

While specific curriculum areas have been identified in these materials, some of the materials found within them are of value across different curricular areas, and are worth investigating. Indeed, some teacher training programmes have already begun to use these materials to model best practice. However, it is anticipated that current teachers, as well as newly qualified staff, will benefit from these resources. And this is where the subject learning coaches have a part to play: within the curriculum areas listed, they will be expected to take the lead in working to improve and enhance learning and teaching, to pilot the use of the Standards Unit resources, and to provide peer coaching to colleagues.

A SUMMARY OF **KEY POINTS**

During this chapter we have looked at the following key themes:

> The reasons why CPD is important for teachers and trainers in FE.

> The different ways in which CPD needs are identified by individuals and organisations.

> The different activities that constitute CPD.

> The roles of the Standards Unit and the IfL in encouraging CPD within the FE sector.

The FE sector is undergoing a great deal of change at this time: some have described what is happening as the 're-professionalisation' of the FE sector. Clearly, with new professional qualifications, a firm commitment from government to improve learning and teaching within the sector and new, national structures for CPD being piloted, CPD will become a more common feature of the FE teacher's working life. There will undoubtedly be benefits and disadvantages to this approach, and although broader speculation such as this is beyond the scope of this book, it would be a fruitful topic of conversation among both trainee and experienced teachers.

Websites

The following websites have all been referred to in this chapter, and are worth looking at:

www.ifl.ac.uk
www.successforall.gov.uk
www.subjectlearningcoach.net

Journals

For those who wish to read further, the following journal articles are recommended:

Kennedy, A (2005) Models of continuing professional development: a framework for analysis, *Journal of In-Service Education*, 31 (2), 235–250

Shortland, S (2004) Peer observation: a tool for staff development or compliance?, *Journal of Further and Higher Education*, 28 (2), 219–228

Books

Mentoring is an area of increasing interest within FE, and those who are interested in mentoring are recommended to look at:

Wallace, S and Gravells, J (2007) *Professional development in the Lifelong Learning Sector: Mentoring*. Exeter: Learning Matters

5
Working with others: collegiality and collaboration

By the end of this chapter you should:

- understand the importance of collaborative work with other tutors, other professionals and other organisations;
- be aware of the benefits that a collaborative approach can bring to the professional work of the tutor;
- be able to identify appropriate opportunities for engaging in relevant work in collaboration with fellow professionals;
- be aware of potential professional dilemmas when working with other professionals.

Professional Standards

This chapter relates to the following Professional Standards:

Professional Values:

AS 5 Collaboration with other individuals, groups and/or organisations with a legitimate interest in the progress and development of learners.

Professional Knowledge and Understanding:

AK 5.1. Ways to communicate and collaborate with colleagues and/or others to enhance learners' experience.

AK 5.2. The need for confidentiality, respect and trust in communicating with others about learners.

Professional Practice:

AP 5.1. Communicate and collaborate with colleagues and/or others, within and outside the organisation, to enhance learners' experience.

AP 5.2. Communicate information and feedback about learners to others with a legitimate interest, appropriately and in a manner which encourages trust between those communicating and respects confidentiality where necessary.

Introduction: making room in the staffroom

A quick scan of the titles of some books and journal articles relating to new teachers in the learning and skills sector reveals, for example: 'no good surprises'; 'in at the deep end'; 'new teachers' survival guide'. And there are lots of others. Everyone knows that being a tutor is not an easy job, but all these titles seem a bit negative, don't they? Surely everyone, or most people at least, feel a bit trepidatious when starting a new job? Is working in a college so very different?

One important aspect of becoming a professional tutor is the nature of the relationships that we establish and develop with other people. The way that we work with our learners is of paramount importance, of course, and is a theme that comes up time and again throughout this book. But we also need to think about the ways in which we work with other members of staff at colleges, training centres or adult education institutions. This might include other tutors in the same or other departments, or managers, ground staff or learning support workers.

The ways that these relationships are established can be quite different. On speaking to some of my current and former Cert Ed/PGCE trainees, it would appear that experiences of being a new tutor vary considerably.

- **Some new tutors attended formal induction events at their new place of work. This included meeting staff from a number of departments, including support staff, a tour of the buildings, and being given some practical help (for example, where to find the photocopiers and the coffee machines). Managers would take an active role in helping the new tutor to settle in.**
- **Some new tutors arrived in their staffrooms on their first day and were left to simply get on with it. Sometimes, a friendly new colleague would help out, but this was not always the case, and the first few hours or even days sometimes proved to be overwhelming. Managers might offer help, but would be difficult to track down.**
- **Some new tutors found it very difficult to establish good working relations with other tutors, because of their working patterns. Evening class tutors, especially those who only worked on a part-time basis, often felt cut off from other colleagues, including their managers.**

Meeting new colleagues who turn out to be supportive and genuinely helpful is a great help to new tutors, who often feel silly or embarrassed about asking questions that 'everyone knows the answer to apart from me': further education colleges, in particular, are busy, complicated organisations with many rules and procedures that only really are acquired over time and through practice. Having a mentor to help navigate a new workplace, though, is often a luxury.

Relations with colleagues are not just a focus of attention for new tutors, however: longer-serving, established tutors often draw on the help and experience of their colleagues in a number of ways.

- **Tutors who have little knowledge or experience of working with learners with disabilities can seek out guidance and support. At times, we will need to speak to and receive help from other members of staff who have specialist skills, qualifications and experience in providing the help and facilities needed by learners in these situations.**
- **Tutors who are less than confident in using IT equipment in the classroom can gain help from technicians, or other staff who can provide both practical help (for example, in setting up a data projector in a classroom) and more detailed help (for example, the use of a particular IT application).**
- **Tutors who want to try something new with a group of learners can talk to other tutors who work on the same, or a similar, programme of study. A fresh pair of eyes is often helpful, and a colleague could provide suggestions for a trial run of a new learning or teaching strategy.**

Building relations with other members of staff in other departments takes time and effort and some people are better at it than others. It isn't only new members of staff who get stuck over a particular problem and need help from elsewhere. And there are plenty of longer-serving tutors who have forgotten somebody's name or occupational role.

Similarly, professional relationships may extend beyond the confines of a particular institution:

- **Some colleges have establishments in a number of locations and, as a result, staff from different sites may rarely meet. Tutors who work on community-based outreach courses such as adult literacy and numeracy courses or family learning programmes may find that a community-based environment works in a very different way from the 'main site' of a college.**
- **Tutors from different education and training providers, but who teach on the same or similar courses, may meet on a professional basis. This might be for a moderation or standardisation event, or as part of a CPD programme.**
- **Some colleges have working relationships with HE institutions, running HE courses on a franchise basis, or offering progression routes to HE as part of a collaborative widening participation initiative. Other colleges have close ties to industry and business, and work closely with employers in their region.**

Being a tutor is a far from solitary occupation, therefore: whether being asked for a reference or being asked to design a new programme of study, our work, as tutors, by necessity involves other people in addition to our learners: colleagues, other tutors in other establishments, employers and other stakeholders. This is not to deny that for some tutors, feeling that they are at the fringes of institutional life is a feature of their working lives: part-time tutors often miss out on CPD, for example (as discussed in the previous chapter); outreach tutors may not always work at the main site of a college. Relationships with colleagues and other professionals – tutors, managers, employers – can work across a range of departmental, institutional and geographic boundaries. These themes will be considered in more detail shortly.

Theory focus

Team membership styles

Chapter 8 includes a brief analysis of learning styles, and if a learning styles approach is unfamiliar, then skipping ahead is recommended. Similar approaches are to be found in management theory, and relate to the different qualities that individuals bring to a team in the workplace. Psychometric or personality trait testing based on models such as the Myers–Briggs personality type theory or the Belbin team role theory is commonly found in industry, less so in the education and training sector. Such models assume that individuals have different capacities and characteristics, and that a balance of such qualities is needed for teams of people to work successfully together. For example, some people are good at detailed, fine-grained work, and others are better at seeing the bigger picture. Some people are good at procedural work, and others are good at critical and evaluative thinking.

Do you think that the people that you work with in your subject or curriculum team have a balance of complementary qualities? Or is it the case that you collaborate with your colleagues so infrequently that you are not really aware of how they work?

Defining terms: collaboration and collegiality

Before continuing, it is important to define the key concepts that make up the title of this chapter. 'Collaboration' is the more commonly found word of the two, and in this context, it refers to the act of working together with one or more people in order to achieve a particular goal or set of goals. 'Collegiality' is, perhaps, a word that is encountered less often. In this context, a collegial approach to something is one based on the notion that the different people involved all have an equal status: there is no overall leader. A collegial approach seeks to encourage a sense of shared responsibility and shared effort, of meeting the organisation's goals through consensus.

Working with other tutors

REFLECTIVE TASK

REFLECTIVE TASK

As you read the following journal extract, think about your own first day as a tutor or in your current post: this might have been in a large further education college or a small community education centre. How did it feel when you went in on that first day? Who did you talk to first, and did that initial meeting make a lasting impression on you? If you are currently working towards a teaching qualification and have not yet taken up a post, focus on your teaching placement as you consider these questions. Ask your mentor how they felt on their first day.

In this journal extract, Jo, who completed her teacher training on a full-time basis, looks back on the placement that she undertook at a large further education college. She teaches business studies, having come from a management background.

> My first day: it was months ago, but I can still remember it really clearly. We had had some presentations in class about what our placements might be like, but you can never really know because the different colleges that we all got sent to were so different in terms of size, or location, or the kinds of courses offered there. Some of our tutors were really positive, and stressed that we would get lots out of it if we worked hard, but others were really negative and said that it would be a real culture shock and so on. I'm not sure that kind of message helped.
>
> From the front, it looked great, but all the new buildings were by the road. I was in the old sixties' block near the car park. It was pretty scruffy, but okay. The classrooms were all really different. Some were great – really tidy, posters up that must have been done by the learners, laid out in seminar style. But some were dreadful – scruffy, in rows, it just looked like no effort had gone into making them nice places to work in.
>
> The staffroom. So untidy! Some desks were spotless, and some were covered in junk. There were only two computers, and I counted 10 desks, one of which had a note on it saying it was mine. I sat down, looked around, and had no idea what to do next.
>
> But then Daniel came in, and he was great. He said hello and we got talking and he told me some useful things – practical stuff really. He told me how to get a computer network password, where the resource files were for the unit I was teaching, and he was generally friendly. In fact, I always got on with him much better than I did with my mentor, who always seemed to be rushing around. I think Daniel's calmer approach settled my nerves and helped me take a breath.

For new tutors, or trainees who are on a placement, the initial contact can make a lasting impression, and this need not be with a mentor. Daniel's friendliness and his practical advice helped Jo settle in to her new role. Jo will still have had much to learn, but knowing that she could ask for help was undoubtedly reassuring.

While writing this chapter, I asked one of my current teacher training groups about the things that they wished they'd known or asked about on their first day as tutors. A number of issues were raised, including:

- **where to get resources made up – such as photocopying, transparencies;**
- **how to get computer and library passwords, and where to get IT kit from for use in class;**
- **where to find all the official forms that need filling in – registers, enrolment forms for learners – and where to send them once they were completed.**

This is not to say that once a tutor has settled in, the need for help or cooperation simply dissipates. The establishment of good, and friendly, working relations with staff can be seen as operating at a number of levels.

- **A tutor might need help with something relatively straightforward, such as how to use a particular piece of equipment, or the loan of a piece of equipment or resource.**
- **If tutors are willing to share ideas and materials, then this might cut down repetition. If two tutors collaborate when preparing a body of materials or freely share their resources, then the overall effort expended is less. And at the same time, they can evaluate each other's work and offer feedback.**
- **If tutors are faced with a serious professional dilemma, perhaps related to the behaviour of a learner or the pressure caused by having to deliver a particular course, being able to talk over these dilemmas can be a relief, and may lead to ideas for new approaches or strategies to deal with the issue.**

In one sense, therefore, such collaboration can be seen as a highly pragmatic and sensible way of working: the working life of a tutor in the learning and skills sector is characterised by busyness: there's a lot to do, and never enough time in the day to do it all (or, at least, that's how it feels sometimes). If some of that effort can be shared out, then it must be to the advantage of everyone.

Another way of thinking about such collaborative ways of working is in terms of the profession as a whole. The learning and skills sector, and further education colleges in particular, have embraced market-led reform over the last 15 years. A business ethos dominates working life in colleges. The nature of the tutor role has also changed over this time, and some of the ways in which the tutor's job has been redefined were explored in Chapter 1: these included such diverse responsibilities as recruitment and publicity, and pastoral support. As the job of the tutor becomes more diffuse, a collaborative approach can be seen as being a necessary component of the role: a new aspect of professional behaviour. We shall return to this issue in the following chapter.

It is worth remembering that there are also opportunities to work with tutors from other institutions. It is always pleasant to meet tutors who work in different places: they might have ideas for learning and teaching that are unique to them, and their experiences, perhaps due to the size or location or specialism of the institution in which they work, may be informative and helpful. But such opportunities are unevenly distributed: in some curriculum areas, cross-college work, for example for the purposes of moderation or standardisation, is a regular feature. Other curriculum areas simply do not offer the same kinds of opportunities.

The part-time tutor

And finally, the experience of the part-time tutor needs to be considered. For a full-timer, or a part-timer with a substantial contract (say, three days a week), opportunities for networking with others are relatively easy to find. For a part-time tutor who comes into an adult education centre for a couple of evenings a week during term-time only, the experience of work can be a lonely one: administrative or support staff often don't work into the evening; resource centres may not be open (if they are available at all); technical staff are rarely available to help if the data projector doesn't work. How can a part-time tutor feel part of an organisation when their experiences seem to be so marginal? Similarly, for those who combine a tutoring or training role with a broader area of professional activity, for example in nursing where a teaching role may be only a small part of a professional repertoire, it may be difficult to find other professionals to network with who are also involved in training.

This is not an easy question to answer: if a tutor simply 'isn't there', then they can hardly begin to build working relationships with colleagues. But there are opportunities: staff development events can offer part-time tutors the chance to work with their full-time colleagues (but this isn't necessarily a straightforward process, as discussed in the previous chapter). As we shall see in the following section, it is important for part-time tutors to work closely with their managers, and this can help alleviate feelings of professional isolation.

Working with managers

RESEARCH FOCUS RESEARCH FOCUS **RESEARCH FOCUS** RESEARCH FOCUS **RESEARCH FOCUS**

In a journal article published in 2002, Sue Wallace explored the experiences of trainee lecturers as they undertook teaching placements at further education colleges. When talking about college management, they tended to characterise the relationship between lecturers and management as being divided. The trainees questioned the extent to which management recognised that there was an academic aspect to their work, and noted the lack of integration between teaching and management staff, even down to the relative qualities of their different staffrooms.

A lot of research has been carried out concerning the learning and skills sector and, more specifically, the ways in which the FE sector has become more business-like, akin to the private sector, following changes in the sector in the early 1990s, when colleges passed from local government control to incorporated status. College management teams, in general, have received both plaudits and brickbats from different stakeholders. On the one hand, the best colleges are well run and highly effective. On the other hand, college management teams have been partly responsible for effecting significant changes in the working conditions of tutors who, as was discussed in Chapter 1, now have to carry out a range of duties in addition to 'just' teaching. It would be difficult to deny that the job of a tutor is a busy and demanding one. Nor can it be denied that the profession has changed over the last 15 years, and will undoubtedly continue to do so in the future. But there is no turning back: employees in many different organisational contexts have a very different working life compared to 15, or indeed 50 years ago.

This book does not condone the worst excesses of college management. Nor does it condone the nostalgia of some longer-serving tutors who yearn for conditions of service that will never return. Rather, it promotes a pragmatic response, particularly where relationships with college managers are concerned: it is not the case that they necessarily deliberately set out to make the life of the tutor a difficult one. If tutors have a clear understanding of what their managers can do for them, and if they 'manage their managers', then the impact on the working life of the tutor can be beneficial.

In reality, the amount of meaningful contact that many tutors have with the senior management team of a college is minimal. Tutors are more likely to work closely with middle managers: curriculum or department heads, who normally themselves have been tutors and maintain a teaching role in addition to their management responsibilities. For a full-time tutor, or a tutor with a substantial part-time contract, regular management meetings should be expected as a standard feature of working life. For a part-time tutor in the adult education sector, contact with a department or section head may be more sporadic, especially if the tutor only works outside office hours. In this case, formal line-management meetings are essential, as more informal contact may be impossible, although part-time tutors may find that they are scheduled to meet with their managers on a less frequent basis than their full-time colleagues.

What can a tutor expect from their curriculum or course manager? At a regular meeting, the issues raised might include:

- **the opportunity to discuss how well the tutor's actual teaching is going;**
- **appraisal, or review of a probationary period if a tutor is newly appointed to their post;**
- **the opportunity to discuss possible CPD activities (as explored in detail in the previous chapter);**
- **the chance to discuss any problems or difficulties that the tutor has encountered.**

It is important for tutors to maintain realistic expectations of this process. These issues are far from uncontroversial in various ways, and can be seen as reflecting those aspects of the FE workplace that are most closely associated with a private-sector approach. The following case study provides a more in-depth look at some of the dilemmas raised.

CASE STUDY CASE STUDY CASE STUDY CASE STUDY CASE STUDY CASE STUDY

Staff appraisal

Observation of teaching is a common feature of the learning and skills sector. In addition to Ofsted inspections and those lesson observations carried out during teacher training, colleges frequently hold internal observations of teaching, invariably following the Ofsted common inspection framework as a way of maintaining consistency, and an observed session would be graded. College-based observers should normally be provided with appropriate training. But if the observed tutor felt that, for example, the grade given was too low, an appeal should be possible.

How would a tutor react if they were observed by a member of the college management team who did not have a teaching qualification? This is a not-unheard-of occurrence: compulsory teaching qualifications for the learning and skills sector have been in place for less than a decade. How would a tutor react if they were observed by a member of the management team who had not had significant recent, or relevant, teaching or training experience? An observer with a background in teaching adult learners can hardly be qualified to observe a group of 14–16 year old learners, can they?

The observation of teaching sessions is something of a flashpoint in the relationship between tutors and managers. Some tutors invariably see the process as intrusive, needlessly bureaucratic and as a challenge to professional autonomy. Other tutors see them as a necessary evil or perhaps resign themselves to a ritual that has to be performed at certain times of the year. Tutors do have some say over how they are carried out, most notably in those colleges that operate a policy whereby tutors can nominate which session is observed. And it is worth remembering that even Ofsted inspectors give some warning. This can lead to what might be termed a 'beauty pageant' approach: the observed session can be primped and preened to maximise the chances of a good score. Perhaps, in order to ensure a more realistic approach, observations should take place without warning? Why not, if the tutor is well prepared, to a high standard?

Of course, it all depends on how 'well prepared' and 'high standard' are defined: definitions of quality in learning and teaching are contested, and a management perspective may not be quite the same as a teaching perspective. Quality assurance more generally, of which the lesson observation process is a part, is perhaps the most visible aspect of the business model of FE which stresses performance management through a whole range of procedures such as observations, self-assessment reports and learner questionnaires. Some tutors feel threatened by such constant surveillance. Other tutors resent these procedures simply because of the time that they take to complete, when there are more important things to be getting on with, such as preparing resources for a lesson. Sometimes it almost feels as if college managers simply don't trust tutors to get on with their work. So how can tutors and managers get along in a more collegial fashion? How should tutors work with their managers to ensure that everything gets done, despite the fact that their priorities do not always match?

1. Accept the job for what it is

Seemingly endless form-filling is frustrating: if it's any consolation, managers have to do lots of paperwork as well. In many ways, bureaucracy is an inescapable aspect of many working environments, not just educational establishments. Tutors need to make sure that they know exactly what they have to do and by when, and agree dates with managers and stick to them.

2. Ask managers for help

Sometimes, issues crop up that are beyond the remit of a single tutor. It might be a disciplinary problem with a learner, or an academic concern. If things go wrong, or unexpected problems occur, ensuring that they are dealt with through the correct use of the correct procedure is vital.

3. Make the system work for you

If a lesson observation needs to be scheduled, tutors should talk to the observer in advance if at all possible. Instead of playing safe, why not put the observation to good use, try something new, and ask the observer for feedback?

Although at times it may not feel that way, the majority of managers do in fact want tutors to be both happy and effective in their work, and will help and support them. At the same time, it is worth remembering that many middle managers in particular are as busy, with as many different roles to perform, as tutors. If this is the case then tutors, whatever their contractual status, need to be diligent in ensuring that regular, scheduled meetings take place.

Working with other professionals

During a busy working month, a tutor may well come into contact with a range of other professionals: managers, administrators, learning support workers or employers. Invariably, the focus for such contact is a learner or group of learners, and there are several reasons why it might be necessary to work with others.

- **If a tutor lacks the expertise or confidence to help plan for learning for a learner with a disability, then a learning support worker can be consulted (this issue is discussed in depth in Chapter 9).**
- **If work placements need to be organised for a group of learners on a childcare programme, for example, then a number of employers may need to be contacted in order to provide sufficient opportunities.**
- **Learners on a construction programme may benefit from site visits of varying kinds: good relations with local employers can help make this a straightforward process. Such visits may not be a required part of the curriculum, but they are a good opportunity for learners to experience new things, and provide further links between a college and its community.**
- **Many employers, such as plumbers or electrical contractors, sponsor their employees as they take part in training. In situations such as this, employers will have a strong interest in their employees' progress.**
- **Tutors often have to liaise with awarding bodies. This might be for a relatively straightforward procedure, such as ensuring that a learner is enrolled on the correct programme. Or it might be for a more complex reason, such as organising a form of differentiated assessment for a candidate with specific learning needs.**

It goes without saying that courtesy, efficiency and good organisational skills are all the kinds of personal qualities that can help a tutor in such situations. And for the most part, such activities can be seen as facets of a developing professional repertoire. Occasionally, however, they can be more challenging. Sometimes something may occur that causes inconvenience, such as an employer being unable, after all, to provide a placement opportunity or a site visit despite having promised to do so. At other times, something that seems quite innocuous can have unforeseen consequences. In the following journal entry, Carl, a tutor in electrical installation, reflects on a meeting with his curriculum manager.

> *I had asked to speak to Bill following a telephone call from one of the big contractors' firms. Basically, these guys are paying all the fees for their staff who need to have the updated certificates before they can go out on site. Plus they are coming in on day release so there's a lot of money tied up in them. Normally it all goes fine, but as they're coming to the end I guess the employers want to know what's happening. And this is what I wanted to talk to Bill about, because I don't know how much information I'm allowed to give them.*

> *Bill reckoned that I should say something like 'you've got nothing to worry about' and just leave it like that. He didn't say whether it was confidential or not, but he said that if I was still in industry and was paying for three apprentices to do their certificate, wouldn't I want to know how they were getting on? I said I would, and it's fair enough I suppose. I'm not sure how I'd react if one of the trainees was heading for a fail, though, because they'd have to tell their employer themselves.*

Carl's situation is potentially fraught with professional and ethical dilemmas. On the one hand, he has a duty to the learners, to respect their privacy and the confidentiality of their progress records. On the other hand, the employer will want to know how the trainees are doing, not only because of the immediate financial costs, but also because the smooth running of their business might be affected if the staff do not all possess updated qualifications that meet industry standards. This is particularly important in occupations where qualifications are regulated by government. So how should a tutor act in such situations? Carl provides an example:

> Bill went on to tell me about how he dealt with a couple of trainees who kept skipping sessions. He was concerned to cover his own back as much as anything, which is fair enough, and didn't want their employer turning round and making a fuss if they didn't complete. And then of course it looks bad on your end-of-year numbers if too many people drop out or don't finish their assessments. So by the time they'd missed a couple of sessions, he phoned up their employer and asked how they were and if they had been called to work away or were they ill or something like that because he needed to know what to put on the register and this sort of thing. And that way, he told me, the employer would get the hint and have a few words so that next week, they'd turn up and get some work done. And they did!

Carl has done the right thing in deferring to his curriculum manager in this instance: issues of learner confidentiality are important, and are frequently governed by the provisions of the Data Protection Act.

Carl's example revolved around learners who are adults. For those tutors who work with learners who are aged 14–19, quite different professional relationships may arise. Learners who are aged 14 or 15 may still be attending secondary school in addition to attending college: in such cases, contact with the school regarding progress may be necessary. For full-time college learners aged 17 or 18, academic or vocational tutors will frequently have to work with another colleague who has a pastoral role. Such work might include organising a learner's choice of course or programme of study, or the completion of a reference for a UCAS form.

Tutoring on the margins

Part-time tutors occupy a variety of roles within an education or training organisation. Some part-timers, due to the nature of their post, will frequently be called upon to work with other professionals, and despite their part-time status, will be fully integrated into the life and work of the organisation. For part-timers who teach during the evening, or for hourly-paid tutors who only work during term time, opportunities for professional collaboration may well be fewer. Adult education tutors working for a local education authority may well have no professional responsibilities outside of the contact hours that they are paid to deliver, and may be the only people tutoring a particular subject within that organisation.

There are precious few venues for professional networking and collaboration for part-time tutors, but they do exist. As well as some of the activities mentioned in the previous chapter, there is a growing number of web-based discussion groups that may be of help. The Institute for Learning hosts a number of discussion threads for tutors of different subjects. Teaching My Subject is a web-based collection of subject-centred resources for tutors and also includes a discussion forum. Online discussions may not necessarily be a substitute for regular contact with fellow professionals, but they are a useful supplement.

A SUMMARY OF **KEY POINTS**

During this chapter, we have looked at the following key themes:

> **Some of the factors that promote and encourage collaboration with other tutors.**

> **Ways of working with tutors, managers, and other professionals within the learning and skills sector.**

> **Some of the professional and ethical dilemmas that are highlighted by or negotiated through collaborative working.**

When all is said and done, it will always be the case that there are those tutors who are quite guarded, private and tend to plough their own furrow. And there are other tutors who are open, eager to share and to exchange ideas. And the same goes for those people who occupy other positions in the sector. But in a profession where time is precious and where the demands of the workplace are considerable, does it not make sense to work together where possible and desirable, in order to make the working day that little bit less stressful and more enjoyable?

Website

The Businessballs website (**www.businessballs.com**) hosts a comprehensive essay relating to personality theories, types and tests.

Journal

The following article is referred to in this chapter, and is highly recommended:

Wallace, S (2002) No good surprises: intending lecturers' preconceptions and initial experiences of further education, *British Educational Research Journal*, 28 (1), 79–93

6
Defining professionalism

By the end of this chapter you should:

- have a developing understanding of theoretical approaches to professionalism and professional practice;
- know how to apply theoretical understandings of professionalism to different parts of the learning and skills sector;
- have a developing critical awareness of current debates concerning professionalism and managerialism in the learning and skills sector.

Professional Standards

This chapter relates to the following professional standards:

Professional Values:

AS 4 Reflection and evaluation of their own practice and their continuing professional development as teachers.

Professional Knowledge and Understanding:

AK 4.1 Principles, frameworks and theories which underpin good practice in learning and teaching.

Introducing theories of professionalism

During the course of the first two chapters, we explored a number of ideas and issues relating to definitions of 'professionalism' and 'being professional'. We thought about what constitutes a 'profession' and 'professional conduct' in a number of real-world settings. These themes and issues were quite deliberately situated in the real world, and drew on authentic case studies from a number of different teaching and training contexts. In this way, a number of key concepts relating to professionalism could be discussed without primarily drawing on theory and underpinning knowledge. In this chapter, the theory comes to the fore. Spending time on theoretical issues can undoubtedly seem to be a distraction: surely, with any kind of teaching qualification, what is really important is learning how to plan sessions, or deal with disruptive learners, or how to carry out assessments fairly? Why are all these theories needed? Do trainee teachers really need to know about learning theory, or assessment theory, or (in the case of this book) theories relating to professionalism and professional identity?

The simple answer is 'yes'. In part this is because one of the ways in which a profession is defined is through a commitment to a specialised knowledge base, although that may seem to be a rather circular argument: a professional tutor needs to know about theories of professionalism because theories of professionalism state that professionals need to know about theory. Perhaps a more convincing argument is needed, not least because there are many voices calling for the theoretical aspects of teacher training for the post-16 sector to be scaled back in favour of more practical curricula. How to prevent qualifications to teach in the learning and skills sector from being reduced to tips for teachers courses? By making theory relevant and applicable to the real world.

Putting theories to use

1. To explain why things are the way that they are

NVQ assessors talk about underpinning knowledge. When having a professional discussion with a candidate, an assessor would use a number of open and closed questions to assess the candidate's underpinning knowledge, the assumption being that both knowledge and competence need to be evidenced before the candidate's portfolio is signed off. And this is what theory is good for: it helps practitioners to gather together ideas that can be used to explain things that are seen or experienced in the workshop or classroom. The different concepts that are found within the syllabus for teacher training in the learning and skills sector can be used to frame the reflections of practitioners. For example, a tutor might use Maslow's hierarchy of needs (which is discussed in more detail in Chapter 8) as a way of explaining why an adult education group did not seem to be working as well as might have been hoped.

Such an accumulation of ideas, or theories, through reflective practice, through reading and scholarship, even through writing assignments during a Cert Ed or PGCE programme, adds to the tutor's body of expert knowledge. And it is important to remember that adding to this body of expert knowledge can take place at different times: in the workplace; during a programme of teacher-training; or in conversation with a colleague.

2. To justify a course of action or experimentation

It is to be hoped that tutors are ready and willing to experiment: to do new things with and for their learners. There are plenty of anecdotes in circulation concerning the ossified tutor who has been recycling the same activities and handouts for the last decade and more without revisiting them, but hopefully such tutors are in a minority. By staying fresh and involved, drawing on new ideas or new technologies, tutors can maintain the interest and enthusiasm that they need to do their job well.

But new ideas need context: they need to make sense as part of a broader approach taken by a practitioner. If a tutor is to try something new, some kind of hypothesis must surely be necessary in order to justify the approach being taken. In an audit culture climate where performance is monitored and inspections are rife, the temptation to 'stick with what you know' is understandable. But experimentation, if informed by theory, can be made more reassuring than it might otherwise be.

3. To provide ideas and concepts for exploration

Ideas can be used to try out something new: they can be used to drive practical action in the workplace. However, theory can also come first: that is to say, rather than using theory to inform practice, theory can in itself become the primary focus of the exercise. It's a bit like having a really good toolkit. The more tools tutors have at their disposal, the more tasks they can complete. But they can also attempt tasks that, without the tools, would be unachievable. This is not to say that every tool works in every setting: lots of tools are designed for specific tasks and if someone tried to use one for a different task, the tool might get damaged.

It's important not to lose sight of the practical implications of a good theory. But at the same time, it is important to value the theory itself, and to realise that turning a theoretical frame-work into practical action need not be an immediate process.

Where is theory found?

It is important to remember that theory is not solely to be found within the pages of books and journal articles. Theory can be more or less 'official': that is to say, the body of ideas that a tutor develops over time, in practice, constitutes a body of theory as much as a sequence of ideas drawn from a textbook does. How they are developed, and what exactly the tutor does with these theories is another matter; but if a tutor reflects on and evaluates his or her experiences (in the workshop or seminar room, in the staffroom, with other tutors, learning support staff and learners), then he or she is building a body of knowledge, of theory, that can be used in the same way as theories and ideas drawn from books.

Theorising the professions

Why are some occupations classed as professions and others are not? Clearly, the world at large (or parts of it, anyway) is able to draw distinctions between workers who are members of a profession and workers who are not. The question is: is there any rational or scientific basis to defining a profession? Or, to put it another way, is there some kind of way in which a profession can be identified as definitely being a profession, according to some kind of applicable measure?

There have been a number of attempts by different writers to come up with some kind of definitive answer to what makes a profession 'a profession', normally involving a more or less detailed checklist (for want of a better word) of characteristics that need to be applied to an occupation for it to be considered a profession. If a tick can be placed against all of the criteria listed, then it's a profession. Perhaps not unsurprisingly, different writers have come up with different checklists at different times, but there is a certain amount of agreement between them.

Professionalism and expertise

One theme that occurs time and again in literature relating to professionals and professional education and training is the role of expert knowledge. From this perspective, a professional is an individual who provides a service for others (clients, customers, learners) based on expertise: that is to say, the professional knows and can do things that the client can't do, but needs to have done. This expert knowledge is a specialised body of knowledge, in the sense that it is often quite narrow, perhaps highly technical, and certainly something of a mystery to the client. The only people that the professional could talk to about this knowledge are other professionals, often using specialised language and technical terms that are unique to that profession.

So far so good. But the customers may need to be protected from sharp practice, or from incompetence. How can the professionals be trusted to use their specialist knowledge, which the customers do not necessarily understand, with probity? One way is through the accreditation of specialist knowledge: qualifications. If a professional has the correct qualification, then the expert knowledge is bound to be in place. Nonetheless, ideas about accountability have changed over time: once, it was acceptable to let professionals police themselves, and the formation of professional bodies with codes of conduct was one way of doing this. Nowadays, more formal, external accountability is the norm: for tutors, external inspections and audits help the customers to have faith in the service provided.

Theory focus I: Houle's model of professionalism

In a book published in 1980 Cyril Houle, an American academic and educationalist, proposed a list of 14 characteristics of professional education:

1. Clarifying the defining function of the profession
2. A mastery of theoretical knowledge
3. The capacity to solve problems
4. Use of practical knowledge
5. Self-enhancement beyond professional specialism
6. Formal education and training
7. Credentialling
8. Creation of a subculture
9. Legal reinforcement
10. Acceptance by the public
11. Ethical practice
12. Penalties
13. Establishing relations to other occupations
14. Establishing relations to clients.

To what extent do you think that these characteristics apply to being a tutor in the learning and skills sector? Do you think that they might also apply to occupations that are not seen as being 'professions'? Do you think that an approach such as this – a checklist for professionalism – is a useful or valid exercise?

Some of these issues are easily understood from the point of view of a tutor. Formal training, through working towards a Cert Ed or PGCE, is a well-established feature of a tutor's professional life. And these qualifications act as credentials in the workplace, proving that the tutor knows how to do their job, reinforced by their adherence to relevant LLUK professional standards, which helps provide public acceptance. Ethical practice is enshrined in both the LLUK standards and the IfL codes (as discussed in Chapter 3). And the requirement for CPD in order to maintain QTLS (as discussed in Chapter 4) embodies the need for self-enhancement beyond professional specialism.

Theory focus II: Millerson's model of professionalism

In a book published in 1964, Geoffrey Millerson put forward a model of professionalism that focused on two specific professions: law and medicine. It is perhaps not a coincidence that these two occupations have been seen as professions for a long time, perhaps for as long as 500 years. Millerson's characteristics of a profession are:

1. The use of skills which are based on theoretical knowledge
2. The receipt of education and training in those skills
3. A competence to practise which is accredited by formal examination
4. A code of professional conduct
5. A commitment to the 'public good'.

In an article published in 2001, in a wide-ranging exploration of the different ways in which people working in FE defined professional conduct and professionalism, Ros Clow argued that being a teacher in the further education sector was not a profession according to this model. However, since this article was published, a number of actions within the sector have been carried out: the implementation of first the Fento and then the LLUK standards; the formation of the Institute for Learning; the publication of *Equipping our teachers for the future*. Does being a tutor in the learning and skills sector today meet Millerson's requirements for a profession?

Item 1 is catered for by the initial teacher training curriculum: all relevant teacher training qualifications include theoretical as well as practical elements. Items 2, 3 and 4 can be quickly confirmed: the receipt of an appropriate professional education, a licence to practice and a code of conduct are all now well-established features of the learning and skills workforce. All new tutors have to work towards achieving QTLS, and existing tutors are encouraged to do so through appropriate CPD. Item 5 is perhaps more difficult to pin down: practitioners with QTLS subscribe to both ethical components of the LLUK standards and the IfL code of practice. However, does subscription to a professional body (as discussed in Chapter 3) guarantee that the individual subscriber has actually read the relevant code of practice?

So it might seem that Millerson's model works now in a way that it didn't in 2001. This could be taken as representative of the professionalisation of the learning and skills workforce: tutors once weren't part of a profession, but now they are. This is fine as far as it goes, but there are still areas for debate. An acceptance of Millerson's model, or of Houle's model for that matter (or any one of a dozen others), relies on an acceptance of a number of key concepts that, it could be argued, are not entirely straightforward.

The relationship between education and training, and professional practice

Is doing a teacher training course really related to actually doing some teaching? Or, to put it another way, does doing a teacher training course actually help someone to become a teacher, or does it simply teach someone 'how to do a teacher training course'? Why and how does writing a number of academic essays train people to be better teachers?

> *... there is little immediate transfer of learning from one context of use to another. Using an idea in one context does not enable it to be used in another context without considerable further learning taking place. The ability to use certain ideas about teaching in academic essays or school documents does not greatly increase the probability of being able to use those ideas in the classroom.*
>
> (Eraut, 1994, p33)

There is more to teacher training than just writing essays, of course. Pre-service trainee teachers spend a considerable amount of time on a teaching placement; in-service trainee teachers are already in paid employment on a part-time or full-time basis. This real-world experience provides the authentic context within which the practitioner's skills (along the lines of those set out in the LLUK standards) can be developed. And there is a considerable body of educational theory to suggest that such engagement with real practice is the most effective way of genuinely learning something (situated cognition and communities of practice are discussed in Chapter 8). But if professionalism demands theoretical expertise as well, then ways of blending theory and practice are necessary. This could be through the writing of essays, or through reflection on practice (which is discussed in the following chapter).

Professionalism and managerialism

To be fair, it could be argued that it is naïve to expect that a single and uncontested definition of professionalism should be able to trip off the tongue and be applied to a tutor in an adult education centre or FE college. It is the job of academics to pick apart these concepts and explore their different meanings and implications. For the purposes of this book, some sense that there are definite characteristics to professional work, even if they can't be agreed on by everybody at the same time, is what is important. There is scope for debate, but there is also, at the same time, a professional paradigm: a pattern to definitions of professionalism. And there are other ways to approach the concept: instead of defining it from the ground up, it can be explored in opposition to other ideas and concepts. One way of throwing notions of professionalism into relief is through an analysis of an alternative paradigm: managerialism.

What is managerialism?

To some extent, the clue is in the title: it's all about management, and the importance of management. More specifically, managerialism implies a need for management as a discrete, separate function within an organisation. The activity of management helps the organisation in question to be as productive as it can possibly be, in as efficient a way as possible. The impact of managerialism in the learning and skills sector can be seen as working in two ways. To some extent, it is a reflection of broader trends in the service and manufacturing industries more generally, particularly in respect of the private sector. But in the main, the impact of managerialism in the sector has been linked to the incorporation of FE colleges in 1993. With a private-sector, free-market ethos in place (and there is an assumption that private-sector management is better, more efficient and more responsive than public-sector management), managerialism in the learning and skills sector provides managers with the responsibility for, and the authority to, plan, carry out and then evaluate the service being provided: education and training. According to this model, learners are customers, commodities even, and need to be serviced as efficiently and effectively as possible.

It is not too difficult to tease out areas of tension between professional and managerial paradigms. A professional approach would place the learner at the heart of the teaching process, but not worry about the amount of income generated by that learner. If a learner fails or drops out of a programme of study, a tutor would want to reflect on why this might have happened from a pedagogical perspective, but would not necessarily worry about the financial implications. A tutor would demand learning and teaching resources on the basis of a professional judgement as to what is needed to maximise pedagogical effectiveness; a managerial response would be to provide resources on a value-for-money basis and to ask tutors to 'make do and mend' where possible. A tutor might define their professional competence around their subject specialism; a managerial approach would define the tutor as a flexible worker, and if a tutor were needed in a different curriculum area, would not hesitate to move staff across.

The Lifelong Learning sector: more than just FE

A lot of recent research has focused closely on the experiences of tutors working in the further education sector (and some of this research will be referred to shortly). However, the broader concept of the learning and skills sector goes beyond FE colleges. The learning and skills sector also includes:

- education and training provided in the workplace;
- commercial training, both in-house and for external clients;
- public- and private-sector training, again both in-house and for external clients;
- community learning, including family learning programmes and youth work;
- adult education, provided by training providers, voluntary organisations or charities.

To what extent does the managerialist ethic have an impact on these other areas of provision?

CLOSE FOCUS CLOSE FOCUS **CLOSE FOCUS** CLOSE FOCUS **CLOSE FOCUS**

Teachers, trainers and tutors

Read through the following three pen portraits, each of which provides a brief description of a tutor working in the learning and skills sector. Answer the following questions in relation to each portrait:

1. Is the tutor a professional, according to either the Houle or Millerson definition?

2. What are the factors that might influence each individual's own definition of themselves as a 'tutor'?

3. Is a tutor such as this more likely to respond to or be informed by a professional ethic, or a managerialist ethic?

Portrait One: Jenny

Jenny has been working in adult education for nearly 10 years. She teaches exercise and Pilates classes in a number of different settings: three of her classes are paid for and delivered at a hospital, as a form of palliative care. Two of her classes are funded by the local education authority, and are delivered in a community education building attached to a local secondary school. And two classes are organised by Jenny herself: she organises the advertising, finds and books the venue and plans the delivery of the class according to her own specifications. She completed a 7307 further and adult education teacher's certificate eight years ago.

Portrait Two: Idris

Idris is a tutor in law at a large further education college: he spent several years working in a private legal practice as a solicitor, but found that due to his family commitments, moving to a teaching career would be greatly beneficial. He took up a full-time, permanent post a little over a year ago. As well as teaching, he has course leadership responsibilities which include liaison with the qualification awarding body, admissions to the course and coordinating the work of two other tutors (collating marks from assignments, liaising over deadlines, and so on). He is currently working towards a PGCE in post-compulsory education.

Portrait Three: Rob

Rob works for a county council. Management is his main job role, and he is well qualified in this area, but he also has a teaching role: he is responsible for part of a much larger programme of in-house training. Courses are delivered to county council staff on-site, and are accredited by national awarding bodies. Normally, the equivalent of half a day a week would be spent teaching. Rob has been working at the county council for many years, and has had a teaching role for eight years. He has no teaching qualification.

A number of issues arise from these case studies. Some of the things that you might have thought about include the following.

- **Jenny has a teaching qualification, but it is out of date, and does not map onto the Fento or LLUK standards. When she did her 7307, there were no Fento standards. Which parts of the Millerson model does she not satisfy?**
- **Rob has a small teaching role, but no teaching qualification. Do you think that he would define himself primarily as a teacher, or as a manager? Which parts of Houle's model might not be satisfied here?**
- **Idris has moved from one profession to another. He is a qualified solicitor but not yet a qualified teacher. With which profession do you think he might associate himself?**
- **Question 3 above, which raises the issues of professionalism and managerialism, is perhaps the most slippery. Jenny, for example, might well try to recruit as many learners as possible to those two classes which she runs herself: she runs these classes on a self-employed basis, and the learners represent a part of her income. Is she more or less likely to limit the class size for pedagogical reasons rather than for reasons to do with the size of the venue?**

It is, of course, a highly artificial exercise to label one tutor as being a managerialist, and another as a professional, and to assume that the values attached to each are entirely incommensurable. Is there anything so wrong with a commitment to public forms of accountability (the managerial ethic) as opposed to a form of accountability that is carried out behind closed doors (the professional ethic)? Similarly, it is difficult to assume that one professional identity can be quickly acquired and another left behind. Can an individual maintain a commitment to the values and standards of two professions, or more than two? Can different codes of practice be reconciled?

Exploring professionalism

Ideas about professionalism are a lively source of research and debate. A number of suggestions for reading appear at the end of this chapter, and what follows draws from these sources. It is important to note that much of this research focuses quite specifically on the FE sector, although many of the issues raised can be considered in other contexts. The ways in which professionalism is defined and understood can be said to be influenced by a number of factors.

1. The conditions under which tutors in the sector are employed, and the actual conditions under which tutors work

How many tutors are full-time, and how many are part-time? Is being a part-time tutor a good thing, because it allows an individual to maintain other career plans or interests, or is it a bad thing because it leads to the creation of a divided workforce, with full-timers receiving different treatment to part-timers? Are tutors expert professionals or flexible workers? In many FE colleges, contracts of employment do not specify the actual subject that the tutor will teach (an issue discussed in Chapter 2). It is not uncommon for tutors to find themselves teaching courses that they feel less than fully qualified or prepared to deliver.

> *Early research in the field associates FE professionalism with practitioners' former trade and occupational identities that find expression in the instrumental and pragmatic culture of FE. More recent evidence indicates, however, that this prevailing culture is being challenged as residues of old and new FE cultures sit alongside one another ... a paradigm shift is taking place reflected in the emergence of a new 'learning professional' working across academic and vocational divisions, in a more polycontextual environment ... A recurring contradiction identified in the research literature is that traditional forms of professional socialisation and work practice sit uneasily with the multi-skilled nature of FE practitioners' work, in an increasingly performance-driven environment.*
>
> (Gleeson et al, 2005, p449)

For Gleeson et al, the key issue here is the changing nature of the FE workplace over the last 25 years or so. One of the consequences of the incorporation of FE colleges and the subsequent growth of private-sector management and values is this change in the nature of the tutor, as worker. Tutors are no longer viewed as experts based on a craft or trade background, either by others or by themselves. The nature of the FE workplace is so different from how it used to be, that different kinds of tutors are needed. And in a way, the changing nature of the FE workplace is symptomatic of broader changes to people's working lives in all other kinds of occupations. At this point in time, the virtues that are stressed are flexibility, a willingness to adapt, constantly underpinned by reminders that there are no longer such things as jobs for life, and that the UK has to keep up with the global market.

2. Changes made to professional qualifications for tutors, and the impact of professional competences

Over the last 10 years there have been two major reforms of teacher training for the learning and skills sector, neatly summed up by the Fento standards, and then the LLUK standards that superseded them. A number of other initiatives, driven by the DfES, have made a material impact on the sector: Success for All; subject learning coaches; Ofsted inspections of teacher training provision in the sector; mentors. Defining professionalism in these times may be far from straightforward, but the DfES clearly has a particular vision of how it wants the workforce to look: a standardisation of professional qualifications; a licence to practise; adherence to a particular body of professional competences.

FE teachers have long argued that they should be accorded the same professional status as teachers in the school sector, although more often than not this argument is reduced to one of parity of pay and conditions. And perhaps the introduction of QTLS is intended to mirror QTS in the primary and secondary sectors. But the comparison is more complicated: school teaching is a graduate profession and FE teaching is not. The conditions of work in schools are quite different from those in a college: FE tutors are flexible, cross-skilled facilitators; school teachers are subject-based experts. FE tutors routinely work outside normal office hours. Newly qualified school teachers are given a lighter teaching load during their probationary period, together with comprehensive mentor support. Mentors for trainees in the learning and skills sector, at the time of writing, are unpaid, acting in a purely voluntary manner. Many tutors in the learning and skills sector continue to be employed on a part-time, short-term basis, irrespective of the professional qualifications that they may or may not hold. Are the two professions of school teacher and learning and skills tutor at all comparable, or are they different kinds of professionalism?

3. The ways in which tutors themselves think about their role and their work

What do the practitioners think about themselves, the ways and places in which they work, and the people they work with? The models of professionalism discussed earlier both had something to say about the professional's relationship with the people with whom they work. Managerialism may place a premium on efficiency: what do professionals value?

> *Our trainees felt that students had an entitlement to a valid educational experience, one that developed their potential to the full. Trainees implicitly recognised structural patterns of social inequality as reflected in school under-achievement and urban deprivation. They acknowledged that education should recognise difference, and this rested alongside an ethic of care and respect. Our trainees emphasised the need to create pedagogic contexts in which learners felt valued and were thereby empowered to learn. They were critical of practices that marginalized learners and that contributed towards learner underachievement.*
>
> (Avis and Bathmaker, 2004, p7)

Avis and Bathmaker's research was carried out among trainee FE teachers, as opposed to qualified practitioners. But if these are the perspectives and philosophies being carried into the learning and skills workplace, then it would seem to be the case that a model of professionalism is being constructed and adhered to where a wider concern for the learner, rather than a focus solely on performance, is of importance and value.

On the other hand, it could be argued that the creation of contexts within which learners felt valued and empowered to learn should hardly be seen as noteworthy or surprising: isn't that what tutors are supposed to be doing? And the answer is: 'yes'. But what Avis and Bathmaker make clear is an awareness, at least among the trainee teachers with whom they spoke, of broader social and economic factors that have disadvantaged some of the young people with whom they would be working, and a commitment to try and overcome the effects of these.

REFLECTIVE TASK

Go back over the three issues that have just been discussed. As you re-read them, pause for reflection and note down some of the ways in which the themes raised help you to make sense of your own professional practice, and the attitudes that you and your colleagues carry into it. To what extent do you feel that your contractual status, for example, allows or hinders particular kinds of work with your learners or in the organisation at large? To what extent do you draw on an understanding of broader social, economic or political issues when making sense of the challenges of the workplace, whether it might be a disruptive group of learners or a lack of sufficient resources? How do you reconcile yourself to these difficulties?

It is frustrating at best to be faced with a group of learners who are disruptive, who do not value the learning opportunities that they are given, and who seem intent solely on receiving their £30 EMA payment. Being aware of the fact that they might come from a socially deprived background, or a family or culture that does not value education and training, is of scant compensation when another lesson or workshop has been disrupted. So why worry about these background issues? Tutors are not in a position to do anything about them, are they? Probably not: it is the responsibility of policymakers to put substance behind the rhetoric when they talk about the potential of education to create greater social and economic equality. But tutors do need to know about them, if only to draw some comfort from the fact that if a group of learners is failing, it is not their fault. But will the managers see it that way?

This is not to say that all learners in the learning and skills sector are marginalised, excluded or generally difficult. Most are not. For adult education tutors, such issues relating to behaviour are rare, although not unheard of. Perhaps for adult education tutors, attention needs to focus on other issues to do with constructions of professionalism: expertise, qualifications, as well as a commitment to learners. For the part-timer, it is the very fact of being part-time that can be professionally marginalising. And for both full- and part-time tutors, other aspects of the current world of work are unavoidable: performance management, inspection and, above all, a lot of paperwork.

A SUMMARY OF **KEY POINTS**

During this chapter we have looked at the following key points:

> The value of theory as a form of expert knowledge.

> Models of professionalism and how they might be applied to real-life contexts.

> Managerialism, and its impact on tutors in the learning and skills sector.

> Current research relating to the ways in which FE tutors in particular consider themselves to be professionals.

There is a lot more to be said about this: a thorough exploration of theoretical and research-driven constructions of professionalism could fill a whole book. And it can seem abstract, and a bit detached from the real world of work. But a critical appreciation of the values and ideas that we bring into our work need not be a fruitless or purely theoretical exercise: it can help us make sense of what we do and why we do it.

FURTHER READING FURTHER READING **FURTHER READING** FURTHER READING

Eraut, M (1994) *Developing professional knowledge and competence*. Abingdon: RoutledgeFalmer

Houle, C (1980) *Continuing learning in the professions*. San Francisco, CA: Jossey-Bass

Millerson, G (1964) *The qualifying associations: a study in professionalisation*. London: Routledge

Journal articles

Avis, J and Bathmaker, J-M (2004) The politics of care: emotional labour and trainee further education lecturers, *Journal of Vocational Education and Training*, 56 (1), 5–20

Clow, R (2001) Further education teachers' constructions of professionalism, *Journal of Vocational Education and Training*, 53 (3), 407–419

Gleeson, D, Davies, J and Wheeler, E (2005) On the making and taking of professionalism in the further education workplace, *British Journal of Sociology of Education*, 26 (4), 445–460

7
Reflective practice

By the end of this chapter you should:

- **understand why reflective practice is an important aspect of a professional approach to teaching and learning in the learning and skills sector;**
- **be aware of different practical and theoretical approaches to reflective practice;**
- **be aware of appropriate strategies for encouraging reflective practice.**

Professional Standards

This chapter relates to the following Professional Standards:

Professional Values:

AS 4 Reflection and evaluation of their own practice and their continuing professional development as teachers.

Professional Knowledge and Understanding:

AK 4.2. The impact of own practice on individuals and their learning.

AK 4.3. Ways to reflect, evaluate and use research to develop own practice, and to share good practice with others.

Professional Practice:

AP 4.2. Reflect on and demonstrate commitment to improvement of own personal and teaching skills through regular evaluation and use of feedback.

AP 4.3. Share good practice with others and engage in continuing professional development through reflection, evaluation and the appropriate use of research.

Thinking about reflective practice

There is a good chance that this is not the only textbook related to teacher training for the learning and skills sector that you will have come across. As such, there is a good chance that you will have encountered the concept of reflective practice before now. If you have not yet done so, you will soon become acquainted with reflective writing, looking at your teaching and your learning through this lens of reflective practice. There are a number of books that are solely about reflective practice. And other professions, as well as tutors, draw on reflective practice: nurses and social workers, for example.

Put simply, there's a lot of reflective practice about. Perhaps there is too much. It can be confusing for some, and perfectly straightforward for others. Some tutors find the process of reflecting on their teaching practice to be a genuinely eye-opening experience, leading them to consider and evaluate aspects of their work that they had not thought about in any detail before. Others find the process mechanical and lacking meaning, a distraction from what they perceive to be their main role as a practitioner in the workshop or seminar room. Champions of reflective practice will point to the fact that as a professional activity, it helps tutors to make sense of what they do and to value the knowledge and experience that they gain in the classroom to the same extent that they value the knowledge gained from books or journal articles. Critics of reflective practice argue that it is a highly subjective process that should be kept at a personal level, and shouldn't be read or assessed by another.

The purpose of this chapter is not to present an uncritical appreciation of reflective practice: like just about anything to do with teaching and training, it has good and bad points, and works well for some and less well for others. What we will do is try to think about how, in the real world as well as during a programme of tutor training, it can be a useful tool, among others, for the professional's work.

What is reflective practice?

This sounds like a straightforward question, but the answer is in fact complex. For some practitioners, reflective practice is a state of mind, a permanent kind of behaviour. In this sense, being a reflective practitioner involves a constant, critical appraisal of teaching and learning, and of the work of a tutor more generally. Reflective practice is a way of exploring and picking apart all those aspects of teaching that get taken for granted. This outlook becomes a permanent part of the tutor's professional repertoire, as important to professional identity as a clutch of specialist qualifications: reflective practice is as useful and valuable a way of learning as reading a book or journal is.

For other practitioners, reflective practice is a bit of a chore at best and a waste of time at worst, especially during a programme of teacher training. It's a repetitive exercise in navel-gazing, something that doesn't need to be written down and certainly shouldn't be assessed or graded by a teacher-training lecturer. It is criticised as being a subjective process, perfectly worthwhile for individuals who choose to engage with it, but certainly not something to share or transmit.

There is no denying that as soon as anything becomes compulsory, it can become a burden. Reflective practice is no exception. I have worked with and spoken with many tutors from the learning and skills sector and on many occasions, having described reflective practice to them, I have been met with comments along the lines of: 'I do that anyway. Why do I have to write it down?' The simple answer is: 'because you have to as part of the assessment requirements of your tutor training qualification', but this is a far from satisfactory response. So how best to encourage reflective practice?

Reflective practice in action

When travelling home on the train after teaching an evening class, I would sometimes (but by no means always) take time to think over how the class had gone. I always found this to be useful: being on the train gave me some quiet time, with few distractions, and I would think about the work that my students and I had done that evening. Sometimes it would be very simple, practical issues that came to mind: I had tried to cover too much content during the session and had been forced to rush things, for example, or the handout was hard for a couple of people to read because I had used a small font in order to squeeze it onto one side of A4. At other times, I would think about individual members of the group: perhaps, during a small-group activity, one or two members of the class hadn't seemed to have taken much of a part in the activity. And then I would start to think about why this might be: were they finding the course harder than expected? Had I explained the activity with sufficient clarity? Should I rearrange the groups and get different learners working together? I didn't know that this was one kind of 'reflective practice' until I did my PGCE a few years later and had the term introduced to me. I never used to sit down consciously and think to myself, 'now is the time to think about how my class went this evening'. It just happened sometimes.

The point of this story is pretty obvious: I was reflecting on aspects of my teaching practice. It was essentially a technical kind of reflection, focusing on particular problems or dilemmas that were to do with how a specific teaching session went. But for me, and for many of the learners in teacher training classes with whom I have worked, this is where reflective practice starts, as a way of evaluating what worked well during a teaching session, and what worked differently from the way I had planned it. It seemed to be a natural process, 'something that I do anyway', and to make sense as part of a professional approach to teaching and training: a good tutor is always thinking about how the session went, what might need changing for next time and what worked well so that it could be tried out elsewhere.

Even if this kind of technical reflection is almost instinctive, moving beyond the technical to a more thoughtful and critical kind of reflection might not be. And this is where professional study, normally during a course of teacher training, can help, because there is a lot more to reflective practice than just thinking over the layout of your handouts.

REFLECTIVE TASK

Read the following extract from the learning journal of Helen, who is coming to the end of her tutor training course. As you read, think or make notes about the kinds of issues, relating to her learners, that she is writing about.

> *I am still obsessing over handouts. At the start of every term, I tell my learners that the best way for them to learn is to write their own notes during class and then use the textbook for additional information, but by the end of term it's always the same: all they want to do is to have paper copies of the PowerPoint slides and if I don't provide them, they all complain and I have to send an email with the PowerPoint attached to keep them happy! I end up doing this nearly every week. I know why they work this way – it's easy and takes less time. But the assignments are only ever full of stuff that comes from the handouts, and I'm not sure that they are doing enough additional private study.*

This is only a short extract, but there's a lot to unpack here. Let's take a look at the different issues raised.

As tutors, we invariably have our own ideas and beliefs about learning and teaching. These ideas come from different places: teacher training courses; our own experience; the experience of friends or colleagues (and different ideas about teaching and learning will be discussed in the following chapter). Helen's desire to encourage her learners to write their own notes rather than simply rely on class handouts is a laudable one. There is evidence to suggest that learners do indeed learn better from making and then reading their own notes. At the same time, it is difficult to escape from the prevailing 'handout culture' that surrounds us. Learners and trainees have come to expect a particular level of service from tutors: they are often paying for education or training as a service, after all. Trainees and learners in all kinds of contexts (adult education, work-based training, colleges) expect to receive handouts, or other printed materials, produced to a high standard. So, who's right: should Helen stand her ground because she knows what is best for her learners? After all, she is an experienced and qualified professional. Or should she provide lots of handouts because that's what her learners expect and, depending on the course, have paid for?

There is another possibility, of course: some of her learners may work best, and learn best, from printed materials, not from notes that they have made themselves. Some of them may work best by making notes on the printed handouts. And some may prefer to take notes in class, and then to read through the handout later on as a revision or reinforcement exercise. Without subscribing to a particular approach to learning styles (a controversial topic at best, and one which is touched on in other chapters), it must be right to say that different learners do like to do things in different ways. Shouldn't Helen, as a professional, try to accommodate these preferences? This is a loaded question, of course, as the answer is bound to be 'yes'. Helen has her own understandings, theories and convictions about the learning and teaching process, and that's fair enough. But if she had reflected more critically on her approach to the class handouts, and had been more willing to challenge her own assumptions and preconceptions, she might have been able to see things from the learners' point of view.

So how might Helen proceed? One suggestion might be for her to think creatively about the handouts that she is currently providing. If her aim is to get the learners writing, why not provide handouts that encourage this? Simply printing off the PowerPoint slides doesn't leave much scope for activity: too many handouts end up being filed away, unread, or simply thrown away. Redesigning the handouts from scratch, to encourage the learners to write on them, might be a good way for Helen to make them more useful. There are a number of strategies that she could employ: she could create gapped handouts for use during a formative assessment activity. Or she could deliberately create handouts that simply summarise key points from her PowerPoint slides, rather than reproducing the slides in full, and encourage learners to annotate them during the session.

This case study draws on a number of issues: Helen's professional knowledge and experience; what she has learned as a tutor and what she has learned during her programme of teacher training; what she expects of her learners, and what her learners expect of her. If Helen is going to get anything really useful and permanent out of this, she needs to reflect critically and systematically on how she has approached the issue of the class handouts. Rather than simply giving out handouts and then moving on, she needs to think about her whole approach to handouts, and perhaps make changes to not only her practice, but also what she understands, what she knows, about this aspect of the learning and teaching process. Or, to put it another way, she needs to revisit and change aspects of her professional knowledge.

Reflective practice and professional knowledge

It is its relationship to professional knowledge and practice that makes reflection such an important aspect of the professional's repertoire. If reflective practice were to remain at a technical level, restricted to the evaluation of teaching strategies and resources, then it wouldn't deserve the prominent place that it does occupy. But if we use reflective practice to explore critically the assumptions and preconceptions on which we base our training and teaching practice, we can build on our understanding of learning and teaching and enhance our professional knowledge. Such an approach to reflective practice makes certain assumptions, which aren't without their problems, and can be argued over, but are useful nonetheless.

1. We can learn from our experiences

The relationship between experience and learning is by no means a straightforward one, and there are a number of different theoretical approaches that try to explain this. Perhaps the best known model is the experiential learning cycle of David Kolb, which can be found in many tutor training textbooks and DfES Standards Unit materials. In brief, Kolb's theory (and it is a theory, not a fact) states that people learn from their experience, and that the way this happens is through reflecting on the things that we actually do (our concrete experiences) and then, following this reflection, we can experiment in similar situations next time and perhaps have another experience, that we can reflect on in turn, and so on. What is important about this process for now is the role of reflection: we learn from our experiences through the process of reflection.

2. The knowledge and theories that we acquire from our experience are as useful and as valid as the knowledge to be gained from studying or reading

Learning in formal contexts, from books and from courses and programmes of study (and not just teacher training), is valued without question in the world at large: it's a 'good thing', in this age of lifelong learning, to gain qualifications as publicly recognised markers of learning achievement. This is all well and good, but it privileges official, formal learning and neglects the fact that lots of learning takes place outside formal educational settings. We learn from experience, from friends and from colleagues, from trial and error or from something that we have read on a website or in a magazine. Reflective practice provides us with the means to make sense of this learning, to organise it and evaluate it.

3. The knowledge and theories that we acquire and reflect on in some way characterise our work as 'professionals'

In the preceding chapter, we spent some time thinking about different kinds of professional knowledge and competence. One of the themes discussed was the way in which the knowledge and understanding acquired in the workplace are as valid to the professional as the knowledge and understanding gained during study for a qualification.

Theory focus

In a book called *Theory into practice*, published a little over 30 years ago, Chris Argyris and Donald Schön put forward the argument that there are two kinds of theories used by professionals as they go about their work: espoused theories and theories in use.

Espoused theories

These are the 'official' theories of a profession: the ideas that are found referred to in textbooks and manuals, codes of practice and conduct. They have gained an established place in the world of professional activity and as such are passed down to new generations of professionals during programmes of study that are endorsed by the professions in question. Whether these theories work in the 'real world' or not is another question.

Theories in use

These are the 'unofficial' theories of a professional: the ideas and concepts that people draw on, in their professional capacity, in the 'real world' of work. We may say one thing in the cold light of day, but when

---

we are in a workshop or classroom, we do another. We generate our own ideas and theories about learning and teaching independently of courses or books.

For Argyris and Schön, these theories are as important and as useful, as 'good', as the official theories. So how do we make the most of them? How do we tease out these theories and apply them to maximum advantage? The answer is: through reflective practice.

Reflective practice: different theoretical frameworks

If reflective practice is such an important professional activity (or skill, or technique), then how do we actually go about doing it? Having established a rationale for reflective practice, we need to think in detail about how it's done, and this is where things can get confusing because there are a number of different theoretical frameworks to look at. Some of these ideas do overlap, but there are some differences as well. This complexity is both a strength and a weakness: it's a strength because it shows that 'reflective practice' is a lively area of debate and critical engagement that isn't standing still. It's a weakness because with lots of different theories to choose from, 'reflective practice' runs the risk of being seen as confused in itself and confusing to practitioners.

There are many books and journals all about reflective practice, and it would be a difficult task to try to sum them all up here. We have already referred to David Kolb, and the role of reflection in the experiential learning cycle. What follows is a necessarily selective summary of some of those other approaches to reflective practice that are more commonly found in the learning and skills sector. Here, three different writers are briefly discussed, and a number of others are quickly mentioned. There are some similarities between their ideas, but some differences as well.

John Dewey: reflective thinking

John Dewey was a leading philosopher and educationalist. He wrote extensively on a range of issues, not just education. For the purposes of this chapter, however, our interest lies specifically in Dewey's concept of reflective thinking, set out in his book *How we think* (1933), and which has been a significant influence on a number of later writers, including both Donald Schön and David Kolb.

Dewey was interested in solving problems. When a tutor comes across some kind of problem or dilemma, they engage in a process of reflective thinking, leading to learning, that would allow a solution to be found, tried out and resolved. In fact, reflective thinking can only happen in these circumstances. To explain this process more fully, Dewey proposed a five-stage model of problem-solving.

1. Suggestions. During this stage, some possible solutions to the problem that has been encountered are considered.
2. Intellectualisation. During this stage, the problem needs to be defined and a question or series of questions need to be put forward that can lead to a solution.
3. Hypothesising. During this stage, the tutor starts to put together a number of possible solutions to the problem, thinking creatively and imaginatively about how to explain or solve it.
4. Reasoning. During this stage, the solution is carefully thought about and reasoned over, perhaps

involving reference to other sources of information.

5. Testing. Finally, the solution to the problem is tested out, in the real world.

It is important to note, however, that this problem-solving model is not necessarily to be followed to the letter; nor is it always desirable to follow each stage of the sequence in turn. In real life, thinking and problem-solving are never this straightforward. For example, an acceptable or useful way of framing a problem as a question or series of questions may only come about during a process of hypothesising and reasoning, or even after testing out a hypothesis. Tutors may well find, as they solve problems, that they are jumping between stages. Proceeding from one stage to the next in an orderly fashion is not what Dewey is suggesting: rather, it is a process of reflective thinking as a way of solving problems that he is advocating, and it's a process that happens to have five components.

Donald Schön: *The reflective practitioner*

The starting point for Donald Schön's book *The reflective practitioner*, first published in 1983, is that professionals need to know more than they can learn simply from attending a course and gaining a qualification: it is in the real world of professional experience that a different but still necessary kind of learning takes place, and the knowledge that this learning generates is as valuable and valid as the knowledge found in canons of literature. The process of reflection allows the professional to explore their experiences and what they know. But what a professional knows is not just what they have been taught as part of a professional qualification. In fact, sometimes a professional cannot actually say what they know: they 'just do it'. It's in 'the doing' that professional knowledge resides. Schön argues that if professionals can pick apart these things that we know when we do them, then they can be more effective, more creative, more 'professional' in their work. And he proposes two forms of reflective practice in order to facilitate this: reflection-in-action, and reflection-on-action.

Reflection-in-action

Reflection-in-action is the kind of reflection that takes place in the heat of the moment, on the spot. It's the kind of reflection that happens instantaneously, almost unconsciously, as the professional solves a problem or a dilemma. For a tutor, an example might be when a session isn't going quite the way that it has been planned. Perhaps the trainees are more familiar with the topic being discussed than the tutor anticipated. Perhaps some of the IT equipment isn't working properly. Perhaps one or more members of the group are behaving in a way that threatens to disrupt the work of the group as a whole. Reflection-in-action is found in that moment when the tutor, drawing on their experience, knowledge, skills and understanding of this and other situations (what Schön calls the professional's 'repertoire'), changes direction and decides to run the session differently, or to change the planned sequence of activities for that session, or to introduce something new. To the outsider, this might look like the tutor is simply 'winging it' but that is not the case: what is happening is that they are drawing on their accumulated experiences and knowledge to change the direction on the session, responding to the needs of the learner group.

Reflection-on-action

Reflection-on-action is the kind of reflection that takes place at the end of the day, when the dust has settled. This is perhaps a more conscious, deliberative process. With reflection-on-action, Schön argues, the professional needs to think critically about what has taken place, to analyse and evaluate the actions that were carried out, and to consider what might have happened if a different course of action had been chosen. It is a retrospective process, that can be written down or spoken (but doesn't have to be) that can be used by the professional to build or develop their own theories-in-use.

Stephen Brookfield: critical lenses for reflection

In his book *Becoming a critically reflective teacher*, first published in 1985, Stephen Brookfield argued that reflection is something to be encouraged among learners as well as tutors (and encouraging reflection among learners is discussed in the following chapter). For the tutor, which is the focus of this chapter, there are four key perspectives for reflection. That is to say, there are four points of view (called 'critical lenses') that can and should be taken into consideration when reflecting on practice:

1. the point of view of the practitioner – our own perspective;
2. the point of view of our learners;
3. the point of view of our colleagues;
4. the point of view of established theory, as found in relevant literature.

Brookfield is interested in what he terms 'assumptions', those things which we do, and those things that influence the things that we do, that we never really think about or ask questions about. For example, a tutor working in the learning and skills sector might, quite under-standably, be committed to a student-centred approach to learning (and this is discussed in more detail in the following chapter). Such a commitment would obviously influence the tutor's choice of learning and teaching strategies: one commonly found approach is small-group problem-based learning, where the tutor sets the group a task and the learners have to research the problem and report back before the session finishes, or perhaps in the next session. On paper, this approach looks great: it empowers the learners, encourages them to take responsibility for their own learning, and promotes a democratic approach where the learners learn from each other, not just from the tutor at the front of the room. In practice, however, things are not so clear cut: some learners may require a more structured, tutor-led approach; they may not be ready for independent learning. Some learners may see the tutor as shirking their responsibilities, leaving the learners to 'get on with it' instead of doing any 'proper teaching'. And some tutors may indeed employ such strategies because they have not made sufficient preparations for a session.

A willingness to unpack such assumptions, which have powerful advocates in many different contexts in the learning and skills sector (and in the wider education sector as a whole), is what characterises critical reflection. Certainly, reflection can and should focus on the tech-nical, the 'nuts and bolts' of teaching and training. But it should, in this critical form, focus on broader, more profound issues as well: those issues that have an impact on learning and teaching that are to be found outside the immediate confines of a further education college or adult education centre. Brookfield has a concern for the political and the social: those broader forces that do indeed impact on our learners and our teaching. Sometimes, if a dilemma or challenge presents itself, a possible solution (or, at least, a way of thinking about the problem) is to be found not in the immediate context of our own teaching approach, or the institution for which we work.

Evaluating approaches to reflective practice

Having several different approaches to reflective practice to choose from can perhaps be seen as being too much of a good thing: which one to choose? Is one 'better' or 'more correct' than another? The simple answer is that they all have different advantages to offer, and it is a mistake to privilege one kind of reflection over another. There are several issues to consider in this regard.

1. Different approaches to reflection have lots in common

Essentially, reflective practice can always be seen as a process of careful evaluation and questioning: of classroom practice; of approaches to teaching and learning; of one's own beliefs and understanding what learning and teaching should be about.

2. The differences between these approaches can be useful to us as tutors

Brookfield's critical reflection offers something different from Schön's models of reflection-in-action and reflection-on-action. Brookfield explicitly leads the reflective practitioner into a consideration of broad political or social issues that, all too often, are lost sight of. A focus on the immediate classroom context is unavoidable, and the steady pressure for classroom management, carrying out assessment, keeping retention rates high and getting results leaves little time for thinking about the 'bigger picture'. Any approach that makes us think about why the learning and skills sector looks and feels the way it does, is to be welcomed.

3. Different approaches have their own strengths and weaknesses

Several writers have provided cogent criticism of these different approaches to reflective practice. Dewey is criticised for ignoring emotion and the affective domain of learning and reflection; Schön's model is criticised for being vague or unclear: what exactly is the difference between his two sorts of reflection? Can reflection actually happen 'in action' at all? Does the proliferation of different theories relating to reflection simply indicate confusion rather than coherence regarding what it actually is?

For those who are new to reflective practice, or who are going beyond reflection as just a form of evaluation of teaching and learning for the first time, the debates that surround it can be offputting. The study of reflective practice ranges across educational theory, theories of knowledge and competence, and theories of professional identity. However, it is important to stress that a critical engagement with different theories of reflective practice is not needed for a tutor who wishes to reflect on their own practice. The use of one reflective-practice model or another need not imply unthinking or uncritical acceptance of the model in question: it can simply be seen as a pragmatic approach, a way of finding a method of reflection that works best for the individual.

Strategies for reflective writing

The models of John Dewey and Stephen Brookfield are easily adaptable for a wide range of purposes. Although these models were not intended by their authors to be followed to the letter, they do provide useful templates or frames for reflective thought or writing. And there are a number of other frameworks that could be considered, which are referred to at the end of the chapter. What follows is an amalgamation of different writing frames, prompts and comments that is not intended to be a definitive statement on reflective practice, but rather to be an immediately applicable framework for trainee teachers. The assumption is that this process will be written down, after the event, but this is simply because it is easier to revise or review the written word compared to the spoken. It may be the case that written reflection follows on from conversations with friends or colleagues.

A framework for reflective writing

This framework is not intended as a step-by-step programme: not all steps will work for or benefit all people: it is intended only to be a series of prompts.

- Start with the thing that you are reflecting on: here, we shall refer to it as a 'dilemma'. This might be a specific incident in a session such as a learning activity that didn't go according to plan. It might be an issue that has cropped up in subsequent sessions, such as disruptive behaviour. It might be a more general issue, such as low recruitment to a course.
- Have you done anything about the dilemma yet? If your dilemma is an immediate specific incident, how did you respond to it? What actions did you take or might you need to take in the immediate future? Are you capable of taking action at all? Some dilemmas are outside our immediate control.
- Think about the dilemma in relation to your own experiences as a tutor. Have you encountered similar dilemmas in the past, and if you have done, how did you make sense of it at the time?
- Think about the dilemma in relation to your prior and current knowledge as a professional tutor with, or working towards, a professional qualification. To what extent can you draw on other ideas, in books or journals, to help make sense of your dilemma?
- Talk to someone else about your dilemma. This might be a colleague in your staffroom, a mentor, or a teacher-trainer. They may be able to point you in the right direction, or they may be able to help you through the sharing of a similar experience of their own.
- Talk to your learners. Are they able or willing to talk openly about the dilemma?
- If the dilemma is in the past, and you are now looking back, was there anything else that you could have done in that situation?
- If the dilemma is ongoing, is there any action that you can take to resolve it? Do you need to refer to a colleague or manager or other professional, or is this something that you have the resources or ability or need to resolve yourself?

A framework for unreflective writing

This framework is not intended as a step-by-step programme either. You don't have to include all of what follows for a piece of writing to be unreflective.

- Don't complain endlessly about an aspect of your teaching practice (resources, colleagues, learners) without ever taking any steps to change things, or at least to understand why things are the way that they are.
- Don't simply describe lots of things that you have done during teaching or training sessions without evaluating or exploring them.
- Don't engage in self-absorbed contemplation at the expense of the wider world: believe it or not, reflective writing is not only about you.
- Don't think that reflective practice is only about identifying things that are going wrong and then trying to fix them.

> ## A SUMMARY OF **KEY POINTS**
>
> **In this chapter we have looked at the following key points:**
>
> > **What reflective practice is and how it works as an aspect of professional practice.**
>
> > **The relationship between reflective practice and professional knowledge.**
>
> > **Different theoretical approaches to reflection.**
>
> > **Ways of encouraging reflective practice.**
>
> **It must be said that some people do find reflective practice difficult: writing in the first person, using 'I' in the course of an assignment and relying as much on personal experience as on books and journals simply feels 'not quite right' to some. This is fair enough, and the hegemony of reflective practice is perhaps a cause for concern. Is it possible to be a good teacher without being a reflective practitioner? Can a trainee teacher fail an assignment during a teacher training course for not being 'reflective enough'?**

At the same time, it is worth remembering that, as Rita Johnston pointed out in 1995, practitioners were being reflective long before Schön wrote his book, and the danger of his, or of any other reflective-practice model, is that it may become an end in itself rather than a means to an end. Reflective practice helps us to work out what we do and why, but it needs a real-world application. Or, to put it another way, what is important is that, as tutors, we are constantly thinking about what we do and why we do it, and that we don't take anything for granted, whether it comes from teacher training books (including this one), college managers or government ministers.

Websites

Useful summaries and essays relating to reflection can be found at the Encyclopaedia of Informal Education: **www.infed.org**

Journals

For a refreshing critique of reflective practice, the following article is recommended (with thanks to Claire Chatterton for this reference):

Ixer, J (1999) There's no such thing as reflection, *British Journal of Social Work*, 29, 513–527

The following is also recommended:

Johnston, R (1995) Two cheers for the reflective practitioner, *Journal of Further and Higher Education*, 19 (3), 74–83

Books

There are a lot of books on this subject. For those who wish to explore particular perspectives in depth, the following would be good places to start:

Argyris, C and Schön, D (1975) *Theory into practice: increasing professional effectiveness*. San Francisco, CA: Jossey-Bass
Brookfield, S (1995) *Becoming a critically reflective teacher*. San Francisco, CA: Jossey-Bass

Dewey, J (1933) *How we think.* Lexington, MA: Heath

Kolb, D (1984) *Experiential learning.* Englewood Cliffs, NJ: Prentice-Hall

Schön, D (1983) *The reflective practitioner: how professionals think in action*. Aldershot: Ashgate

An alternative approach would to be to go to a secondary source. The following are highly recommended:

Moon, J (1999) *Reflection in learning and professional development.* Abingdon: RoutledgeFalmer

Moon, J (2004) *A handbook of reflective and experiential learning.* Abingdon: RoutledgeFalmer This book contains, among other things, a number of useful photocopiable resources.

8
The centrality of learning and learner autonomy

Learning and teaching: an introduction

An investigation into past and current approaches to and understandings of the teaching and learning process by a historian of education or of education policy is hardly needed in order to appreciate the changes that have taken place over the last 100 years and more. Popular culture is replete with stories and images that illustrate these changes, although relatively few of them are concerned with the learning and skills sector. Nonetheless, some key themes can be drawn out: changes to the way that teaching is carried out (less 'chalk and talk'); changes to the way in which people access education and the numbers who are able to do so (widening participation); and the integration of learners with special educational needs into the mainstream (inclusion). Knowledge, understanding and attitudes relating to education and training practice are almost unrecognisable compared to the ideas and policies of a century ago. Issues to do with inclusion and widening participation, and the considerable professional and ethical issues that they entail, will be discussed in the following chapter. In this chapter, we shall focus on ideas to do with the processes of learning and teaching, how these change our notions of professional practice, and how this impacts on our work with our learners.

REFLECTIVE TASK

Before moving on, spend some time reflecting on your own experiences of education and training. Think about this in terms of being a learner, and of being a tutor (whether in employment or on placement). Think about how you learned and were taught, how you teach now and how your learning (perhaps on a course of initial teacher education) is supported and encouraged. What kinds of ideas or understandings about the learning and teaching process do you think underpin your current experience? And how are these different – or similar – to your experiences in the past?

It's safe to assume that a number of themes and issues might arise from completing this activity: you might have noted that current practice favours a more 'learner-centred approach', for example. Or you might have highlighted changes in the way assessment is carried out as being a significant development in recent years. Changes such as these are driven by a number of factors: a developing recognition of and sensitivity to the needs of different learners, perhaps; or changes in the resources and technologies available to tutors. There is one factor that is always to be found, however, sometimes overtly referred to, and at other times only obliquely drawn on: theory of learning and teaching. Educational theory undoubtedly possesses a chequered history, and there are plenty of examples of changes made to educational provision, influenced by ill-conceived theories, that did more harm than good. Nonetheless, a critical awareness of theory is important. Partly this is simply due to the requirements of the profession: as we discussed in Chapter 6, a sound theoretical knowledge base is a prerequisite of any profession and, by extension, of any professional qualification. But this is also due to the fact that a grasp of theory is a good thing in itself, and provides the practitioner with the 'intellectual toolkit' that they need both to make sense of their practice and to inform new approaches and innovations in their work.

An overview of theories of learning and teaching

Theories of learning constitute a key component of the curriculum for initial teacher education in the learning and skills sector. They are readily found in textbooks, staff development and training manuals and in the CPD resources produced by the DfES Standards Unit. As such, a detailed analysis of all these different models of learning will not be attempted here, because it would repeat a lot of what can be found in other places (some of which are recommended at the end of this chapter). Therefore, some theories of learning will only be briefly referred to. Other theories will receive more detailed treatment, however: many teacher-training textbooks focus on a core of theories, such as behaviourism or cognitivism, and more recent work is hard to find. This section will provide an introduction to other perspectives that, it is hoped, will go some way towards addressing the deficiencies of other models.

REFLECTIVE TASK

As you read the following section on models of learning and teaching, try to bear the following in mind: while it might seem, at first glance, that such theories are irrelevant or remote from day-to-day teaching practice, this is not in fact the case. Much of our professional activity can be explored or reflected on through perspectives such as these. When going through the different theories, think about what each one has to say about, firstly, the role of the tutor; and secondly, the relationship between tutor and learner.

1. Behaviourism and neo-behaviourism

I have put these two versions of behaviourism together since there seems to be some confusion about where 'behaviourism' stops and 'neo-behaviourism' starts. Psychologists of the behaviourist school (John Watson, Edward Thorndike and Burrhus Skinner, to name three) studied animal behaviour in order to help construct a more general theory of human learning. Behaviourist theory is best summed up as 'stimulus–response': that is to say, when a person is exposed to a particular stimulus, an appropriate response can be encouraged through offering some kind of pleasant experience as a reward. And incorrect or undesirable responses can be discouraged through offering an unpleasant experience as a reward (if 'reward' is the right word for it).

These theories focus on observable behaviour, not on what goes on in the mind of the learner. As such, they can be seen as focusing purely on getting a learner to perform an action in a certain way, without necessarily wondering or being concerned as to whether the learner understands why he or she is being asked to carry out the task in that particular way. And this issue highlights one major critique of the behaviourist school: does a behaviourist model actually lead to proper learning, or just thoughtless repetition of a particular pattern of behaviour? Does it adequately describe the acquisition of skill or competence (for it is competence-based learning that has a behaviourist model most frequently attached to it)?

2. Cognitivism

Cognitivist theory is all about the thinking, the process that the (neo)behaviourists never really touched on. Learning is about thinking and about knowing things, not just changes in behaviour. Once again, there are a number of different theories and theorists to draw on, such as Robert Gagné, David Ausubel and Jerome Bruner. In brief, a cognitive model of learning assumes that as learners learn, they draw on and build on the knowledge that they already have, and go on to disregard some of that prior knowledge when it is no longer necessary, or when new learning has made it redundant. This idea is often linked to a broader developmental theory, drawing connections between physical and mental growth: this leads to the conclusion that learning is qualitatively different for adults than for children: the intelligence of an adult is more rigid and less easy to change compared to the intelligence of a child.

So far so good, but these ideas are also open to criticism. The cognitive tradition does a good job of exploring thinking and knowledge, but it doesn't do enough to explain how all this knowledge works in the real world. It assumes both an ideal version of thinking and knowing, and a way of allowing cognitive activity to transfer from one setting to another. And this idea of the unproblematic transfer of learning has profound consequences for, among other things, the organisation of the curriculum in colleges as well as schools. Key skills are a good example: can literacy and numeracy be taught and learned on their own? Or do they need to be embedded in different areas of the curriculum?

3. Humanism

Humanist psychologists such as Abraham Maslow and Carl Rogers focus on the development and self-direction, or motivation, of the individual. Maslow's hierarchy of needs is ubiquitous in teacher training texts, and will not be explored in detail here. Briefly, Maslow assumed that in order for people to do their best, to achieve self-fulfilment, a number of other needs have to be satisfied first, including (in order) physiological needs such as food and warmth; safety needs such as feeling secure both mentally and physically; social needs such as friendship; and esteem needs such as respect. Maslow's model is highly popular, but it is open to some criticism, not least at a common-sense level. To take one example: it is absolutely the case that lots of learning takes place in adult education centres or colleges or workplaces where rooms are stuffy, too cold, or cramped. A strict reading of Maslow would have us assume that learning in such an environment cannot happen. It is a distraction, but not an insurmountable one. On the other hand, notions of a sense of security make more sense: learners are hardly likely to engage in class discussion, for example, if they think that their contributions are going to be trivialised or belittled by their tutor.

Rogers has been highly influential in the post-compulsory sector. His focus on the development of the learner led to a model of learning that explicitly places the learner at the centre of the learning and teaching process. Learners, according to Rogers, should be encouraged and helped, by tutors, to decide for themselves what they need to learn and how to go about it. The tutor's role is to facilitate this learning.

Rogers provides a considerable challenge to established notions of the relationship between tutors and learners. Rather than acting as subject specialists, tutors act as facilitators of a curriculum that can be negotiated by the learner. What the tutor knows, in terms of subject specialism, is not as important an aspect of his or her professional role as is the ability to facilitate learning. We shall return to this issue later.

4. Models of adult learning

A number of writers have put forward variations on the idea that adults learn differently from children. The best known of these is the 'andragogy' model of Malcolm Knowles. In a series of books, Knowles put forward a model of adult learning that rests on a number of assumptions: that adult learners are self-directing; that they draw on their experience when learning; that learning is linked to changes in life and work; that adults learn most effectively when solving problems, rather than learning 'subjects'. Andragogy is perhaps less influential today than it once was, but it still has a resonance for many practitioners.

Again, the model raises a number of concerns, not least at a common-sense level: when is an adult 'an adult'? Are adults always capable of directing their own learning? Do adults always want to be self-directing? Many adult education practitioners have a philosophical commitment to the concept of the self-actualised adult learner, but the reality can be very different. Many adult learners want to be told what to learn, and when. Some adults want to be taught, not 'facilitated'. We shall return to these issues later.

5. Social constructivism

One of the most powerful critiques of behaviourist and cognitivist approaches is that they are often based on experiments that took place in laboratories, rather than the outside world, and that they frequently involved animals, not human beings. To put it another way, what can one of Skinner's experiments, involving a bird in a box pulling a lever to get food, really tell us about the complex processes of learning and teaching that we encounter in our professional lives?

A social constructivist approach helps us with this deficit. Rather than focusing solely on abstract experiments, social constructivism focuses on how processes of social interaction impact on mental development. One leading theorist in this field was Lev Vygotsky, who argued that interaction with people, objects and places, as much as with ideas, was needed for learning to take place, and that the development of higher mental functions was unavoidably linked to social behaviour. Learning takes place in what he termed the zone of proximal development (ZPD). The ZPD is simply a way of describing the time and place when two or more people are involved in a learning activity. On one side is the learner, who may already be capable of solving problems or answering questions at a particular level. On the other side is the tutor. In the ZPD, with the help of the tutor, the learner will be capable of working at a higher level, compared to the level at which he or she can work independently. Eventually, after instruction, the tutor can pull away, and leave the learner working independently at this new, higher level.

Vygotsky also paid close attention to tools, objects or artefacts: after all, much human activity involves using tools of one sort or another. This might refer to an axe, a lathe, a pen or a computer. Vygotsky suggested that learning how to use tools such as these is also dependent on context, and on who else is involved: a learner might be able to work out how to use a tool to achieve a particular result, but a tutor would be able to show the learner how to use the tool to its fullest potential.

6. Social cognition

Another critique of behaviourist and cognitivist learning theories is that they assume that something called 'learning transfer' takes place in a straightforward manner. Learning transfer is defined as the ability of a learner to take what they have learned in one setting and apply it in another. The formal curriculum, delivered in schools and colleges, rests in great part on this assumption. Theorists of social cognition, however, argue that this transfer is far from straightforward. Learning, they argue, is highly context-specific. Solving a problem in a programme of formal learning is hardly the same as solving a problem in real life. How often, in real life, do we have to answer essay-style questions or solve a series of equations? Problems in real life (and this might be the workplace, family life, or something related to a hobby) are rarely written down and presented to us in a coherent package: they often emerge in a messy fashion, and can change or throw up new problems as we work to resolve them. And in real life, there isn't always a right answer or right way of doing something.

In a book published in 1988, Jean Lave wrote about the Adult Math Project in the US. In this project, people who were out doing everyday tasks such as their grocery shopping were observed as they carried out calculations relating to their shopping. Then they were asked to do formal tests. People always performed worse in the formal tests.

7. Communities of practice

One model of social cognition positions learning as a purposeful activity that is situated within 'communities of practice'. These communities are everywhere, and people may be members of any number of different communities. The concept of the community of practice was theorised in depth by Etienne Wenger in his book of 1998 (although first used in a book co-authored with Jean Lave a few years earlier), and a community of practice was defined as possessing a number of characteristics: mutual engagement; joint enterprise; and a shared repertoire.

- **Mutual engagement. In any community of practice, people will work together, in complementary and overlapping ways, at some kind of activity or number of activities.**
- **Joint enterprise. The work of the community is shared, but need not be uniform. Participants in the community will negotiate their understanding of the enterprise and its effects in their lives.**
- **Shared repertoire. Within a community, participants work with a shared repertoire of tools, artefacts, ways of talking and writing, and ways of behaving.**

So where does the learning happen? Wenger draws a distinction between newcomers to a community, and those who have been members for a longer time, and who have gained a greater and deeper expertise. Newcomers can learn from the longer-standing members and from each other. What is important is that learning is happening in an authentic community of practice. That is to say, people learn through participating in practice.

Communities of practice, as originally conceptualised by Lave and Wenger, cannot be created or designed: they simply emerge in practice. In his later book, however, Wenger put forward the idea that a learning architecture could be created that might provide the opportunity for learning within a community. Such an architecture might include the right resources or the right people, for example, but he stresses that there will always be uncertainties between designing a learning architecture, and how it will work in practice. More recent work on communities of practice has focused on industrial and work-based settings, and the idea has continued to evolve.

Professionalism and theories of teaching and learning

The previous reflection focus posed the question: what do theories of learning and teaching have to do with everyday practice in the workshop or classroom? And the answer is: everything. It doesn't matter whether the theories that we draw on are explicit or tacit: they still shape the ways that we work. If we know and understand these theories, we can explore them, criticise them, and see how they affect our work: how we respond to our learners; how we construct our training and teaching sessions; and how we see ourselves, as practitioners and as professionals.

PRACTICAL TASK PRACTICAL TASK **PRACTICAL TASK** PRACTICAL TASK **PRACTICAL TASK**

In the journal extract that follows, Stephen, who is a tutor in business studies, recounts his experiences during the beginning weeks of an evening course for adults. As you read, think about the ways in which his theoretical perspective has informed his approach to the practicalities of learning and teaching with the different groups of learners that he writes about.

> *After another long day with the 16–19 group, I was really looking forward to teaching the adult education group yesterday evening. The younger group are still quite reliant – a bit too much spoon-feeding still, and they aren't yet doing enough private study outside class. They'll get better as the year goes on, but it's a little hard at the moment. Usually, the adult groups are much more self-sufficient and willing to direct themselves, but this group isn't working at all.*
>
> *I had asked them to prepare short presentations – only a few minutes – and had let them loose in the resource centre. After the break when we all reconvened, they did seem a bit quiet – maybe even a bit fed up. And the presentations weren't all that great – pretty bland really. They'd only used a couple of sources and hadn't answered the question. Anyway, I gave them feedback on the spot, and that's when the grumbling started. Basically, they wanted to be spoon-fed, just like the daytime groups. They said that going to do projects in the library was a waste of time, and didn't really help them, and they wanted to know how it related to their assignments. And then they basically accused me of getting them to do all the work, so that I could have an easier time of it before the break! After putting so much time and effort into writing up their project briefs and checking all the resources, I was a bit upset – I don't think that they appreciated how much time had gone in to working it all out.*

Stephen appears to have done everything right for his adult learners group. He has put a lot of work into creating a small project for them, and is understandably disappointed with how the session went. But why did it go wrong? By providing a project-based session, Stephen has provided the group with an opportunity for self-directed discovery learning, quite distinct from the kind of 'spoon-feeding' techniques that he is using with some of his day groups.

The difference is in perception: Stephen perceives his actions as those of a facilitator, an educator who is committed to his adult learners, and who wishes to encourage a meaningful engagement with the subject. Rather than running a tutor-led session, he has tried to get the group to take the lead. However, these learners do not see it that way: their perception is of a tutor who has left them to it when he should be doing some 'proper teaching' (whatever that means). The problem with any learning and teaching approach is that it is the approach taken by the tutor, not the learner. Learners of all ages and in all contexts will have their own perceptions and expectations of their tutors. So, how do these different theories shape our understanding of what it means to be a professional practitioner?

The professional standards listed at the beginning of this chapter raise a number of issues, which can be summarised as: learner motivation; learner expectations; learner autonomy; learning opportunities; and the wider benefits of learning. We shall discuss each of these in turn, in the light of the theories that we have just covered (although it is important to remember that these are very much overlapping factors).

Learner motivation

Thinking about learner motivation raises broader questions to do with participation and engagement with opportunities for learning. Why has a learner decided to follow a particular programme of study? What are the factors that will ensure that learners maintain their engagement with and enthusiasm for a chosen course?

Many of the perspectives detailed above can help us with this. An awareness of the humanist approach concentrates our attention on the need to encourage a mutually respectful dialogue between tutor and learner. A social constructivist approach helps us to focus on the ways in which we support, encourage and talk with our learners as they attempt new tasks or activities. Even a behaviourist approach can help us to think about the ways in which we praise learners for a job well done (although it doesn't particularly help us in exploring why the learners have acted in a particular way, other than in response to such praise). All of this can help us to think about our learners' motivation.

When discussing learner motivation, a number of other issues arise, as framed in the questions posed at the start of this section. It is in the answers to these questions that we find some approaches more useful and practicable than others. The cognitivist school focuses on internal mental activity and does not explicitly address motivation. Adult learning theory in the andragogy tradition assumes that motivation is an inherent characteristic of the adult learner, and does not explore in any depth the consequences of a lack of motivation.

Learner expectations

Meeting learner expectations is, at the time of writing this book, a high-profile component of policy and practice in the learning and skills sector. There is of course an economic argument (if learners don't like what they get, they will vote with their feet, and we looked at these economic tensions in Chapter 2), but meeting these expectations to a great extent falls to the tutors, as the people who will spend the most time with the learners, and who will be largely responsible – like it or not – for the assumptions and attitudes generated by learners during their time on a programme of training or study. But what are those expectations and where do they come from? To some extent, this question is answered by theories of motivation. But there is more to it: ideas about learner expectation are also influenced by a wide range of social factors: government policy; the drive to widen participation; the ever greater need, in work and in life, for formal qualifications. The discussion becomes a little more uncomfortable, however, when it turns to thinking about who really knows best what is good or right for the learner and what they should and should not aspire to.

Let us take one example: providing handouts to learners. The use of handouts is more problematic than it might first appear. As with any learning and teaching resource, the use of handouts should be evaluated carefully.

Is the handout well designed?

A number of essentially practical issues apply here. Font size should be sufficient to ensure legibility, and the use of coloured paper should be considered. It is important to design a handout carefully so that the document is accessible: using large fonts and coloured paper is proven to aid legibility for learners with dyslexia, for example. Other issues that apply to all learners include: is there too much information on the handout? Has an appropriate language register been used?

Is the handout actually necessary in the first place?

This is a more theoretical concern, and not just in the light of environmental issues (a lot of paper gets wasted in the learning and skills sector). The proliferation of handouts, a 'handout culture', has encouraged an expectation that they will always be produced. Learners will frequently ask whether or not they will receive a handout that, for example, summarises the content of a classroom-based session. And tutors feel obliged, perhaps pressurised, to accede to this request. Why are handouts in such demand? Is there any evidence to suggest that they do in fact get read? How many end up in the bin at the end of the day? How many of them are so poorly designed that they are destined for the bin in the first place (for example, a handout to accompany a PowerPoint presentation that consists solely of the slides themselves, six to a side of A4 paper and therefore so small as to be illegible)?

What would happen if the handout wasn't used?

This is the crux of the matter. To what extent are tutors justified in wishing to push their learners into uncomfortable territory? In a social constructivist approach or in a community of practice, artefacts such as handouts can have unforeseen negative consequences. A handout might be misleading or misinterpreted. It might add an extra layer of complication or confusion and cause the learner more problems: put simply, it's another thing for the learner to deal with.

The tutor may have a quite different agenda. He or she may wish to encourage the learners in developing their handwriting, and taking notes in class is an ideal way of doing this. A cognitive approach to learning would support this approach: taking notes, rather than simply reading them, stimulates a higher level of interaction with the material under discussion.

But would the learners feel hard done by? Would they feel poorly served by their tutor? Do they view the provision of materials such as handouts as a value-for-money issue? If they say that they want some handouts, should the tutor provide them, with an eye on the end-of-term evaluation forms, or should the tutor explain why they are neither necessary nor useful?

This discussion has just been about handouts – hardly the most crucial or contested of learner expectations, but a pervasive one. How many times has a group of learners asked 'is this on the handout', as a euphemism for 'do we have to pay attention?' We might usefully expand the debate into other areas: courses that may or may not be 'right' for a learner; the promises for progression that are made to learners; the incentives offered to encourage the take-up of formal opportunities for training and learning. Complex issues such as these are bound up in both a broader professional ethic (as discussed in Chapters 1 and 2) as well as in a particular approach to learning and teaching.

Learner autonomy

'Learner autonomy' is another politically charged and contestable term. It can be found in a range of adult learning theories and humanist theories, as well as in policy statements and sound bites. We read about learners 'taking responsibility for their own learning', 'directing their own learning' and 'managing their own learning', but there is little arguing with the central idea. Learner autonomy is assumed to be beneficial and desirable and, therefore, to be encouraged.

Much theory supports this. In a community of practice, learning happens during the process of engaging in the work of the community, and this engagement is by definition self-directed: members of the community choose their level of engagement (although it is important to note that this need not apply only to formally planned learning activities). Adult-learning models in the andragogy tradition assume that self-direction is an inherent characteristic of the adult learner. The humanist approach defines the tutor as facilitating the self-directed learner. And the influence of these theories can be seen at work in the more general move away from 'chalk and talk' behaviourist approaches to a more involved and learner-centred approach. And at a common-sense level (which is just as important as any academic theory, after all) it seems right to assume that if learners are more centrally engaged in their activities, involved in choices to do with what exactly they are doing, how they are doing it and why, enjoyment and motivation will follow.

At the same time, learner autonomy is a broader professional and ethical problem. If learners are working more independently, where does that leave the tutor? If tutors' professional status is based on expertise, what happens to that status if the importance of that expertise is sidelined in favour of giving more control to the learners? The growth of resource-based learning, for example by using virtual learning environments, may encourage autonomous learning, but requires a fundamentally different tutor role, based less on contact time and more on written resources. For some tutors, this is indeed a challenge to their professional status. But there are many examples in real life of people teaching themselves how to do something: there are shelves and shelves of teach-yourself books in bookshops. If this approach works outside formal education systems, could it work inside them as well?

Learning opportunities

Opportunities for learning and gaining qualifications are undoubtedly diverse, although this is a far from stable factor. Over the last 10 years, by way of illustration, the provision of recreational adult education classes has shrunk quite considerably. At the same time, the provision of numeracy and literacy classes for adults has increased. These are just two examples of changing provision in the post-compulsory sector. Are these changes desirable? The need to help learners improve their numeracy and literacy skills is undeniable and it would be difficult, in the current social and political climate, to argue that funding for such courses should be withdrawn. So why should recreational classes such as local history or millinery receive government funds? Should taxpayers' money be used to subsidise people's hobbies? Of course, the problem is not quite as stark as this, but there are nonetheless some interesting questions to consider. Is there more to learning than just gaining a qualification that will be useful when seeking employment?

Opportunities for learning can be thought about in a number of ways, therefore: in terms of provision of different kinds of programme of study, in different places and at different times; providing financial incentives to study (for example, the Education Maintenance Allowance – EMA); the provision of resource-based learning and drop-in open-learning opportunities; widening participation among social, economic, age, gender and ethnic groups that are under-represented in education and training; recognising the learning that occurs in the workplace. These are the kinds of measures that can open up or encourage new opportunities for learners.

Theoretical approaches to learning and teaching help professionals to make sense of the impact of such measures in a number of ways. The motivation of learners is one; the impact of barriers to learning is another. Humanist and adult-learning models provide practitioners with a number of ways of thinking about the most effective ways to encourage and support those learners who, in the past, have not had a positive experience of the education system. Social cognition and community of practice models provide practitioners with a framework for recognising and exploring the learning that takes place in an everyday setting, which might be in the workplace and which might be informal or even unintentional.

The wider benefits of learning

It stands to reason that there must be more to learning than just picking up a piece of paper at the end of a programme of study. Perhaps there's more to learning than just equipping oneself for the job market. Adult education tutors would certainly agree, especially those who teach on recreational or liberal curriculum programmes. Sadly, such programmes are dwindling in size due to changes in government funding. Much of what practitioners hear from the government seems to indicate that the benefits of participation in the learning and skills sector revolve around work, economic prosperity, competing in the global market-place. The other dominant message seems to be about self-esteem and emotional development, which is highly controversial. Admittedly, both adult learning and humanist models stress the interpersonal relationship between learners and tutors and the importance of the rapport between the two. On the other hand, as discussed in Chapter 3, if practitioners focus on emotional well-being at the expense of new knowledge and skills, what happens to the learning and teaching process? Are we tutors, or social workers? Does the professionals' approach to the learning process allow them to make time for the personal or is the focus solely on passing on new skills and imparting new knowledge?

REFLECTIVE TASK

This chapter is by no means an exhaustive treatment of the issues raised by different theories and models of learning and teaching when considered in the light of the professionalism of the tutor. But it has, hopefully, provided both some accessible examples of the kinds of dilemmas that occur, and some prompts for reflecting on your own practice, and the theoretical models that can help you explore and make sense of it.

A SUMMARY OF **KEY POINTS**

During this chapter we have looked at the following key points:

> The variety of theoretical approaches to the learning and teaching process.

> The ways in which these impact on professional practice.

How to pull these strands together? Trying to round off a discussion such as this can only ever be tentative because there are so many disputed issues to explore. Perhaps it is sufficient, for now, to say that the reason why a careful exploration of theories of learning and teaching is so important for the professional tutor is that it will influence many aspects of our professional work and lives: the ways in which we talk with, or to, our learners; the ways in which we encourage learning; and the ways in which we share, or transmit, or deliver, our expertise and our enthusiasm.

Books

For a thorough account of a range of theoretical approaches, the following are recommended:

Jarvis, P (2001) *The theory and practice of teaching.* Abingdon: RoutledgeFalmer

Jarvis, P, Holford, J and Griffin, C (2003) *The theory and practice of learning.* Abingdon: RoutledgeFalmer

Lave, J (1988) *Cognition in practice: mind, mathematics and culture in everyday life.* Cambridge:

Cambridge University Press

Lave, J and Wenger, E (1991) *Situated learning: legitimate peripheral participation.* Cambridge: Cambridge University Press

Wenger, E (1998) *Communities of practice: learning, meaning, and identity.* Cambridge: Cambridge University Press

Websites

The Encyclopaedia of Informal Education has a number of useful essays on learning theories and theorists. The following are recommended:

Learning theory: **www.infed.org/biblio/b-learn.htm**

Communities of practice: **www.infed.org/biblio/communities_of_practice.htm**

9
Equality, entitlement and inclusiveness

By the end of this chapter you should:

- have a critical understanding of the concepts of inclusive practice, widening participation, and differentiation;
- have developed a critical understanding of how these concepts impact on the professional role of the tutor;
- know how these key concepts can impact on learning and teaching processes;
- be able to reflect on your own professional practice in the light of these key concepts.

Professional Standards

This chapter relates to the following Professional Standards:

Professional Values:

AS 3 Equality, diversity and inclusion in relation to learners, the workforce and the community.

Professional Knowledge and Understanding:

AK 3.1. Issues of equality, diversity and inclusion.

Professional Practice:

AP 3.1 Apply principles to evaluate and develop own practice in promoting equality and inclusive learning and engaging with diversity.

Introduction: widening participation, differentiation and inclusive practice

REFLECTIVE TASK

Before reading on, spend some time thinking about the terms that are listed above. Have you encountered them before, as either a tutor or as a learner? Where have you come across them? What do you think they mean, and how do you think they influence your professional role, if at all?

The terms 'widening participation', 'differentiation' and 'inclusive practice' are commonplace in the learning and skills sector. Perhaps this is a reflection of the fact that the ideas or ethics that underpin these phrases are also, increasingly, commonplace. The further education sector prides itself, rightly, on its work in opening up opportunities for accessing education and training to a diverse population of learners. And while such categorisation is crude at best, nonetheless it is certain groups in society, perceived as having been excluded from education and training, that are increasingly able to take part. So who are these once-excluded groups? Typically, some answers to this question might be: learners with disabilities; or learners from social groups that have, in the past, been under-represented in post-16 education and training. The way that the learning and skills sector works has changed a lot over the last 10, 20 or 30 years, and those learners who were once excluded from mainstream educational opportunity are now accommodated.

There is an increasingly close focus on more conspicuous differences between learners. For example, a partially sighted learner will approach a foreign language course quite differently from a learner with no impairment of eyesight, and will need access to different resources and course materials. Close attention is paid to the specific, individual learning needs of those learners who in the past might have been assumed to be 'just regular' learners, or something similar, and who would have been treated as a fairly uniform group by colleges, tutors and assessors. As a consequence of the acceptance of, for example, a learning styles approach, more careful attention is given to the specific ways in which individuals learn. Tutors cannot treat their group as just one big group of learners: it is a group made up of individuals, who may well need slightly different things from their tutor or their college in order to make the most of their course or programme of study.

There's quite a lot going on here: the body of learners as a whole is more diverse than ever before, and there is an increasingly diverse range of approaches to teaching and learning in relation to them. This, and more, is what is summed up in the terms 'widening participation', 'differentiation', and 'inclusive practice'.

Defining the key terms

- *Widening participation* can be defined as a process by which education and training providers take steps firstly to recruit and then provide ongoing support to learners who, due to their social, economic or ethnic backgrounds or other relevant factors, are less likely to take part in education and training.
- *Differentiation* can be defined as an approach to teaching and learning that both recognises the individuality of learners and also informs ways of planning for learning and teaching that take these individualities into consideration.
- *Inclusive practice* can be defined as an approach to teaching and learning that endeavours to encourage the fullest participation of learners. It also implies a commitment to avoid the opposite; that is to say, it implies that tutors work within an ethical framework that recognises and respects equality and diversity, and the potential for all learners to take part.

So we have three distinct concepts, but there is clearly a significant degree of complement between them: they go together. It stands to reason that a widening participation approach will encourage an increasingly diverse learner population that will embody a variety of different needs as learners, and will therefore require an inclusive approach to planning for learning and teaching. During the remainder of this chapter, I shall use the term 'inclusive approach' as a shorthand for all three of these concepts: by using this term I mean to imply a close relationship between them.

Practical implications

While this chapter consists primarily of an exploration of the professional and ethical issues and dilemmas raised by an inclusive approach to learning and teaching, it is worth thinking about the practical implications for the workshop or seminar room. A comprehensive analysis could fill a whole book, and for more detailed examples and case studies, a number of the references provided at the end of this chapter are recommended. What follows is an account of some of the ways in which an inclusive approach has a real impact, followed by a summary of a more in-depth case study.

- **The ways in which education and training opportunities are actually provided**

An inclusive approach recognises that helping more people to participate in formal education or training requires more than just better publicity for the kinds of courses that might be available at a college of further education or an adult education centre. Of course, spending time and resources in getting the word out about existing provision is a good idea, but in order to widen participation, new approaches to provision are needed. Such new approaches can be modelled in a number of ways. It might involve the provision of an existing course on a more flexible basis: part-time provision might encourage people to take part who cannot commit, for whatever reasons, to a course of full-time study. Evening and weekend provision is similarly employed. Travel to a main campus might be difficult, and so many providers use community or outreach centres of one kind or another so that provision can be offered in a range of local settings. For those who are confident computer users, online learning may be the best option: it offers infinitely flexible, on-demand activity (see below for a more detailed analysis).

At the same time, it is important to remember why some kinds of flexible provision are encouraged, and funded by the public purse, and others are not. At the time of writing this book, great emphasis is placed on, among other things, adult literacy and numeracy. Basic-skills classes can be found in a range of settings at all times of the day. More general adult education is in decline, however: recreational classes are few and far between and those that have survived have done so by moving to a system of accreditation which, ironically, can be a barrier to participation for many adult learners. This is not to say that a concerted effort to improve the literacy and numeracy rates of the adult population is anything other than to be applauded: but surely there is more to education and training than just qualifications? Fewer tangible social benefits, perhaps?

In the following extract, Rory, who teaches art classes to adult learners, reflects on this issue as he starts work with a new class.

The start-of-term panic is over – thank goodness! – and I have got past the minimum number for the course to run: 17 this term. Every year, the numbers get lower, and the numbers I need to run get higher – it was 14 this time. Last year it was only 12. I was chatting to the centre manager, and she told me about how the funding works and how it relates to the portfolios that the learners will produce during the course, but I have to admit that I didn't take it all in.

When the tutors met before term, we had a really good talk about all this: I got on to my usual track about how we should be seen as doing the health service a favour. After all, if these retired people are coming to class, maintaining a circle of friends and keeping their grey cells going, that's saving the government money – no doubt at all. I'll go to classes when I've retired, if there are any left.

Same old arguments about the assessment as well. One tutor as good as admitted that he makes it up so that it looks like all his group completed the tasks. I don't have that problem luckily, as they all produce at least two drawings that can go into their portfolio. And fortunately they tend to be quite sanguine about it – taking a sort of 'well, if that's what it takes to keep the course going then we don't mind' approach.

- **Teaching and learning activities**

An inclusive approach impacts on a tutor's choices of teaching and learning strategies in a number of ways. An increasingly diverse body of learners requires increasingly diverse approaches to planning and designing for learning. The kinds of adjustments that might be made to enable a learner with a disability to take part in a programme of study are a conspicuous example: it is difficult not to notice a note-taker and a British Sign Language (BSL) interpreter working to support a deaf learner. To continue with this example, it is also important to remember that there is more to supporting a deaf learner than just the provision of additional learning support staff. A tutor will need to adjust some aspects of his or her own teaching style as well.

- **Consider altering the pace and timing of activities, so that the BSL interpreter, note-taker and deaf student don't miss anything.**
- **Ask whether notes, handouts or other resources need to be given out in advance. For a deaf student, English is not necessarily a first language. For the same reason, extended library loans may be necessary.**
- **Remember to talk to the learner, not to the interpreter.**

But there is more to an inclusive approach than meeting the needs of learners with disabilities, or specific educational needs. An inclusive approach needs to take account of all kinds of issues that might impact on learners and learning.

- **Have learners had a prior experience of formal education and training that has left a negative impression? Such learners might require additional support to reassure them of the benefits of participation.**
- **Do learners require study skills support? The technical aspects of education and training, such as time management or taking notes, are taken for granted by many tutors, yet many returners to learning lack these generic skills.**
- **Will a diverse group of learners have different preferred ways of learning? Notwithstanding the controversy that surrounds learning styles, and the oversimplistic use of learning-styles questionnaires that verge on the absurd, a variety of activities must be seen as preferable to a single mode of delivery. However, it is important to remember that different subjects or disciplines require particular modes of delivery. A course in electrical installation requires practical skills that cannot be avoided; a course in English literature requires a commitment to reading and private research.**
- **Is a commitment to promoting equality and challenging discriminatory behaviour an aspect of the tutor's professional practice? How should a tutor respond to inappropriate behaviour such as the use of sexist epithets or racist language?**
- **Have learning and teaching strategies been selected and sequenced in such a way that all the members of a group will be able to take part? For example, some learners find it hard to contribute when they are part of a large group, but are more comfortable when working in small group settings.**

Put simply, an inclusive approach might require any number of issues to be taken into consideration: the background of the learners, the social or gender or racial make-up of the learners. In the previous chapter, we considered a range of theoretical frameworks relating to a learner-centred approach. By committing to such an approach, irrespective of the theory that underpins it, a tutor considers each learner as an individual, and plans accordingly, rather than assuming that learners are all the same – they aren't.

- **The use of information and learning technologies (ILT)**

The growth and normalisation of an inclusive approach to learning and teaching have been driven forwards by a number of factors: changing social attitudes; government legislation; changing attitudes among professionals (and this issue will be discussed in more detail below). Another driver has been ILT: as the applications of computers in education and training contexts have become more sophisticated, more straightforward to use and more affordable, so their uses, for the benefit of a more diverse learner population, have expanded. There is something of a chicken-and-egg argument at work here: has an inclusive approach driven technological change, or has technological change made an inclusive approach possible? Either way, the benefits are tangible for a number of different reasons.

- **As an assistive technology, ILT can help learners with a variety of disabilities. Visually impaired learners may be able to read from the screen more easily than from paper, as font sizes and images can be easily magnified. Learners with mobility problems might use a trackball instead of a standard mouse. If writing notes is difficult, speech may be recorded instead. Speech recognition software may help with the production of written work.**
- **Other learners may find the use of ILT beneficial in other ways. For those who are returning to learning, learning basic computer skills can be personally rewarding, for example using email to keep in touch with relatives, or using the internet to investigate family history.**
- **ILT can similarly help tutors to enhance their own practice. Font sizes on handouts can be easily altered. Appropriate resources can be provided for learners in an electronic format. Tutors can use a relatively simple device such as an email group to keep in touch with learners, or use a more sophisticated web-based tool such as a virtual learning environment and set up a message board or a discussion thread.**
- **ILT can help both tutors and institutions to deliver learning resources and courses in more flexible and innovative ways. Distance learning programmes, historically delivered through the use of printed materials sent by post, are increasingly moving towards an online format. More traditional courses can use a blended approach, drawing on ILT use as well as contact time in a college or training centre: a programme that allows a more flexible commitment may be attractive to learners who, for whatever reason, cannot commit to a regular pattern of attendance.**

CASE STUDY CASE STUDY **CASE STUDY** CASE STUDY **CASE STUDY** CASE STUDY

Widening participation in Kent

In an article published in 2001, John Parnham described a widening participation programme in Kent. This initiative, which attempted to engage with adult learners in a specific community which had little access to further education, rested on a number of platforms:

1. a skills audit of the community, in order to find out what kinds of courses would be of use and value to the community;
2. an engagement with other public-sector organisations that provided some time and resources and, most importantly, acted as advocates for the initiative;
3. a development of close relationships with local primary schools, in order to generate more positive images of the benefits of participation in education and training;

4. the acquisition of a new community venue, which would include not only computer-equipped teaching rooms, but smaller rooms for tutorials, a café, a crèche and a drop-in advice centre.

The curriculum was delivered in stages: adults would begin their studies at primary schools, move on to the new community venue, and then progress to the main college campus, following programmes of study of increasing complexity in a number of curriculum areas including numeracy and literacy, IT, and business studies. In this way, adults could gradually become accustomed to taking part in formal education and training with the knowledge that appropriate support mechanisms were in place. This programme was a success, although Parnham reminds us, in the conclusion to the article, that it is expensive.

Professional and ethical implications

These, then, are some of the practical implications and consequences of an inclusive approach. But what about the theoretical issues that underpin them? At first glance, it might seem that time spent wondering about the ethical or theoretical considerations arising from a commitment to an inclusive approach may well be time wasted. The language of inclusion, the policies and government initiatives, the new ways in which previously excluded learners are now supported: surely an inclusive approach is now so uneventful, so everyday, that it doesn't really require, or deserve, any further speculation? Unfortunately, this is not quite the whole story. While the provision of opportunities for learners with disabilities or learners from deprived socio-economic backgrounds is undoubtedly improving, participation in formal education and training is still far from equal, and those learners who come from more advantaged backgrounds do still access education in greater numbers, and with a greater chance of success, than those from poor or minority ethnic backgrounds.

Some aspects of an inclusive approach, such as making reasonable adjustments for people with disabilities, are indeed less controversial than they once were. Other aspects of an inclusive approach, such as the provision of a financial incentive to support the take-up of further education (the Educational Maintenance Allowance – EMA) are more controversial. And yet other issues, such as changes to assessment regimes, are also controversial, but for very different reasons. What follows, therefore, is a discussion of some key dilemmas, of varying magnitude, raised by an inclusive approach.

Establishing a flexible recruitment policy

In Chapter 1, we discussed the issue of class composition and recruitment, acknowledging the possibilities for conflict between allowing someone to enrol on a course based on aptitude, and feeling obliged to enrol someone onto a course for financial reasons. The proliferation of programmes of education and training that do not have specific entry criteria is an important aspect of the widening participation agenda: by providing flexible entry routes, those learners who have not benefited from more formal prior education can still take part in further education. The use of the accreditation of prior experiential learning (APEL) is one method by which the prior experiences of learners, other than formal qualifications, can be recognised as being of merit. At a pre-enrolment interview, a tutor with responsibility for admissions might ask a candidate how aspects of their working or family lives have provided them with the kinds of transferable skills that would be of benefit for a formal programme of study.

Procedures such as these are far from uniformly accepted: APEL is a well-documented educational process, but far from consistently applied. And there are a number of dilemmas posed by an APEL model: do people learn from their experiences? Can the experience of family or working life really be seen as equivalent to a programme of formal training, for the purposes of an admissions policy? Advocates of a flexible, widening participation approach would argue that if someone has the aptitude to make a success of a programme of education or training, their lack of prior educational experience and/or success need not necessarily be a barrier to participation. Many adult education tutors, to pick one example, would be able to tell stories that support this, and many adult learners start from such open-door recruitment policies as this and then go on to achieve considerable success. But the other side of the coin, the feeling of obligation to recruit whoever walks through the door because a line manager somewhere has decreed that without a certain number of learners a class will be closed (and if the tutor is only hourly paid, this closure represents a loss of income), may well lead to the recruitment of some learners for whom, if we are to be bluntly honest, that particular course does not represent the most effective or worthwhile use of their time and energies.

Deciding what is 'reasonable' when making reasonable adjustments for learners with disabilities

Attitudes towards people with physical or learning disabilities have changed and continue to do so, but this is a slow process; sadly, there are many areas of life where discrimination still exists. The additional impetus to allow students with disabilities to access mainstream education comes from government legislation. In 2001, the Special Educational Needs and Disability Act (SENDA) was introduced, and from September 2003, a new section of the Disability Discrimination Act (DDA) came into force. According to this new legislation (referred to as the DDA Part Four), all providers of post-compulsory education were legally obliged not to discriminate against students with disabilities. It should be noted, however, that we might still encounter students who require additional support who are not classified as 'disabled' under the DDA. The Learning and Skills Act of 2001 refers to students with a 'learning difficulty' and we still need to plan our activities carefully to ensure that they are not excluded. According to the DDA Part Four, discrimination against a student may come about in two ways: failing to make 'reasonable adjustment' for a student with a disability; or treating a student with a disability 'less favourably' for a reason related to that disability.

Many of the adjustments that might need to be made for a learner with a disability are relatively straightforward. A partially sighted learner may need access to IT equipment, printed materials with larger font sizes, or a magnifying reading lamp. The arrangement of furniture in a seminar room may need to be altered for a learner who uses a wheelchair. Someone with a mental health difficulty (an unseen disability) may need additional one-to-one support from their tutor because they find it difficult to take part in a whole-class setting. Off-site visits will need to be carefully researched. These are all reasonable adjustments. But can there be such a thing as an unreasonable adjustment? Should all the different opportunities that are offered to people in the learning and skills sector be open to everyone, irrespective of seen or unseen disability?

To some extent, this is a purely theoretical question. A blind learner is unlikely to want to enrol on a stonemasonry course, so any questions about how they will be able, in safety, to access the lofty spires of a Gothic cathedral in order to carry out some repairs can remain unanswered. But what if a blind learner wanted to enrol on a childcare course? This is perhaps more difficult: access to course resources, college facilities and the like can be easily arranged. But what about organising a nursery placement? How would a blind learner carry out a series of observations of the children in their care? Undoubtedly, with the right assistive technology and the right learning support, a blind learner would be able to access most of the learning and skills curriculum, but two questions emerge: are some areas of the curriculum simply off-limits to people with some disabilities; and who should decide, or judge, which areas these are? The answers to these questions are unambiguous: they should be negotiated by colleges and the learners themselves, informed by the same ethos of reasonableness that underpins the DDA.

Providing financial support for learners who enrol at a further education college

The Education Maintenance Allowance is a financial incentive aimed at 16-, 17- and 18-year olds, to encourage them to stay in further education in England. Payments of between £10 and £30 a week, depending on household income, are made directly to those young people who enrol on a course at a further education college, on an apprenticeship, or an E2E programme. In addition, further bonus payments are made to learners who are seen as making good progress and 'do well' on their course or learning programme: measuring such progress can vary between institutions, but tends to revolve around attendance and achievement. The EMA is promoted on the back of statistics relating to educational achieve- ment and employability: nor can there be any doubt relating to the desirability of keeping young people in education and training. If financial pressures are a prime factor in preventing participation, then the EMA would seem to be a good answer. The money is paid to the learner directly, thereby encouraging a degree of autonomy, and there are no restrictions on how the money should be spent.

For some tutors, this is an uncomfortable notion: learners who would otherwise have no interest in staying at college will be encouraged to enrol by the financial incentive on offer, but with no real interest in their programme of study. Once marked as present on the register (a key requirement for receiving each weekly EMA payment), they may disrupt the rest of the group. Put simply, they are only in it for the money. Why not provide similar incentives to adult learners, who are more highly motivated and more willing to work hard towards their qualification? If, however, the EMA offers a significant number of young people a meaningful level of financial support in order to allow them to stay in education or training, surely the long-term benefits outweigh any concerns about the minority of learners who lack such serious intent?

Such arguments cloud the real issues. Before the introduction of the EMA, any group of learners would always demonstrate significant differences in terms of motivation. It could be argued that flexible or open-door recruitment policies have been responsible for many learners coming to classes when, in truth, their interests lay elsewhere. But something does need to be done to break the link between socio-economic status, educational achieve- ment and future employability. The ethical dilemma is not really to do with those learners who treat the EMA as a source of pocket money. Instead, how about taking steps to solve the problems that caused these learners to grow up in deprived settings, rather than simply providing a sticking plaster, in the form of £30 a week, later on in life?

Using learning styles to differentiate between learners

Learning styles are a common feature of working life in the learning and skills sector. The use of learning-styles questionnaires to inform the choice and sequencing of learning and teaching activities is ubiquitous. At the start of many programmes of study, learners are given a 'what kind of learner am I?' questionnaire to complete and the results are used to help the learners to plan and direct their own approaches to learning. As a tool to encourage self-direction among learners, to help them think about their own approaches to learning and to help them 'learn how to learn', such an approach has much in its favour. If learners are to make the most of their opportunities, then it follows that such self-awareness, knowing how and when they work best, must be advantageous. However, learning-styles approaches are often used as a blunt instrument, to satisfy easily the requirements for differentiation that are advocated by Ofsted inspectors and line managers. By showing an awareness of the different learning styles found within a group, and drawing up a lesson plan accordingly, evidence of a differentiated approach can be easily supplied.

Notwithstanding the fact that the proliferation of learning-styles models and questionnaires must surely raise some concerns about how valid and reliable the whole concept actually is, a learning-styles approach does raise some concerns, particularly relating to the specialist knowledge and skills that a course might rest on and demand of the learners who enrol on it. A carpentry and joinery course will always demand a certain level of technical, mechanical ability. A history course will always require reading and research. So the question that emerges is: is a learner-centred approach necessarily the right way to go about things? Should the selection of learning and teaching strategies by the tutor be informed by the learning styles of the group, or by the demands of the body of skills and knowledge that are required by successful practitioners in that particular area?

The answer lies somewhere in between, perhaps. An avoidance of a slavish adherence to learning styles is a far from unrealistic aim. Simple common sense, combined with talking to learners on an informal basis, can help tutors to help learners to think about how they work best. This may be something as simple as studying at a particular time of day, or organising class notes in a different way (for example, the use of mind maps). People do learn differently, but different subjects, or curricula, or technical or mechanical skills require different kinds of practice or work or aptitude: the tutor's role, therefore, should be to bring them together. And if it takes hard work on the part of the learner to acquire a new way of working or learning, then that's what it takes.

Unpacking equality, entitlement and inclusiveness

These concepts do need careful unpacking. APEL-based recruitment or open-door recruitment clearly both have a great deal of potential, but they also encourage pressure to recruit learners in order to fill up courses. Learning styles do help tutors to facilitate a learner-centred approach, and to remember that learning can mean, and be, different things to different people, but they can be used as a simplistic device to demonstrate an inclusive approach, thoughtlessly encouraged by both tutors and managers with little critical appreciation of their merits (or otherwise). Put simply, such issues need evaluating in the light of both other theories of learning and teaching and the experiences of tutors. Or, to put it another way, they need to be evaluated in the light of the professional knowledge, competence and experience of tutors. In addition, they need to be considered in the light of the political, ethical or philosophical commitments of tutors.

A professional commitment to an inclusive approach

How, then, might we characterise a professional commitment to an inclusive approach? How does a commitment to widening participation and differentiation fit in to a broader understanding of the professional role of the tutor? Such a commitment is voiced within the LLUK professional standards, reproduced at the very beginning of this chapter, the Fento standards that they superseded, and the IfL standards that were discussed in Chapter 3. Inclusivity and differentiation are core components of the curriculum for teacher education for the learning and skills sector. They are an accepted part of the body of expert competence and knowledge expected of a tutor in the learning and skills sector. Following this, the next question is to consider how these ideas and commitments found their way into codes of practice and teacher education curricula in the first place. What are the influencing factors that bring an inclusive approach to such prominence? Below are three distinct, though linked, themes that arise from this question.

Legislation and government action

In an immediate sense, it is the direction provided by successive pieces of government legislation that has driven these issues forward. The Learning and Skills Act of 2001 and the Disability Discrimination Act Part Four of 2003 have already been referred to. Looking back over just 10 years, a number of key government papers, reports and initiatives can be identified that have helped to shape the provision of post-compulsory education and training, through, for example, a growing focus on widening participation in further education (*Learning works: widening participation in further education*, published in 1997) and literacy and numeracy (*Improving literacy and numeracy*, published in 1999). In 2001, the Learning and Skills Act came into force, followed by *Success for all* a year after. More recently, *Further education: raising skills, improving life chances* (published in 2006) set out an agenda for reform of the 14–19 vocational curriculum, including the creating of new qualifications and the provision of free level 3 qualifications to all learners aged between 19 and 25.

RESEARCH FOCUS RESEARCH FOCUS RESEARCH FOCUS RESEARCH FOCUS RESEARCH FOCUS

Widening participation is an established feature of college life. Should tutors be concerned about the reasons why it has become more widespread? One research project highlighted the ambiguities that are to be found in the learning and skills sector:

there is some evidence that it is the financial component of widening participation which is providing the catalyst to development rather than the moral/humanistic driver. The resource demand of widening participation means that colleges are being responsive where resources are made available rather than starting from first principles with a review of what the most appropriate strategies may be within their own locality. The moral commitment in the college vision, though, is then translated into an arena of action that is financially motivated. This is excused on pragmatic grounds by some of the senior managers – as the marketing manager of one of the FE colleges indicates 'we are eager to make progress towards widening participation, and we are accountable against our targets – it makes sense to follow the directions that available resources push you'.

(Foskett, 2002, p92)

Does it matter? If widening participation is the result, should we be overly concerned with the details of how or why it has been established?

Changes in professional knowledge and understanding

As a site of research and exploration, education continues to develop in size, sophistication and scope. The growth of provision of courses in 'education studies', alongside a longer-standing teacher training curriculum and a more diverse research base that draws on a range of disciplines (psychology, social psychology, sociology and history, to name four), have led to changes in what learning and teaching, and learners and teachers, are under-stood to be. These issues were discussed in detail in the previous chapter.

Changing expectations of learners, employers and other stakeholders

As attitudes towards disability in society at large have changed, it should not really be a cause of surprise to find these changes reflected in the learning and skills sector. Learners with disabilities (either seen or unseen) are no longer viewed as being 'unsuitable' for further or higher education. Nor do employers view such learners as being unemployable. This is not to say that discrimination does not still exist because, sadly, it does. But changing attitudes are having an impact. Similarly, there is a growing acceptance of the need and value of further education and training in those sectors of society where take-up has, tradi-tionally, been low. Some learners are now more aware of their rights and responsibilities, and seek out relevant opportunities. Employers are keen to reinforce the message that electing to stay in education after the age of 16, or being willing to re-enter education during one's working life, is of significant material and social benefit (as well as being of benefit to their shareholders). The proliferation of advice and guidance centres to help people at all times of life to make informed choices about further education and training also helps to encourage participation.

A SUMMARY OF **KEY POINTS**

During this chapter we have looked at the following key points:

> The issues and ideas that make up an approach to learning and teaching based on an ethos of widening participation, differentiation and inclusive practice.
> Some of the professional debates and ambiguities that are raised by such an approach.
> Some of the practical learning and teaching issues that arise from a commitment to such an approach.

The further education sector deals with an amazingly diverse learner population on a daily basis, and it has shown itself, at its best, to be extremely skilful in doing so. There is still more to do: too many young people still drop out of formal education and training before or at the age of 16, and too many adult learners still shy away from participation. But there has been much good progress since the publication of *Learning works* 10 years ago. Our role, as tutors, is to do what we can to support an inclusive approach, and to pressurise others with whom we work to do the same.

Books

A succinct summary of those recent policy changes that have had an impact on the learning and skills sector can be found in:

Hillier, Y (2005) *Reflective teaching in further and adult education*, second edition. London: Continuum

Journal articles

These two articles are both cited in this chapter and are highly recommended for further reading:

Foskett, N (2002) Marketing imperative or cultural challenge? Embedding widening participation in the further education sector, *Research in Post-Compulsory Education*, 7 (1), 79–95

Parnham, J (2001) Lifelong learning: a model for increasing the participation of non-traditional adult learners, *Journal of Further and Higher Education*, 25 (1), 57–65

Government publications

DfEE (1999) *Improving literacy and numeracy: a fresh start.* London: DfEE

DfES (2006) *Further education: raising skills, improving life chances.* London: The Stationery Office

DfES/NIACE (2003) *New rights to learn: a tutor guide to teaching adults after the Disability Discrimination Act part four.* Leicester: NIACE

Kennedy, H (1997) *Learning works: widening participation in FE.* Coventry: Further Education Funding Council

Afterword

This is by no means a definitive exploration and account of the meanings of professionalism and professional conduct in the learning and skills sector. There are other things that you can read that have more theory in them. And there are other things that you can read that have more ethics and philosophy in them. What I have tried to do with this book is to show how these issues and debates are both relevant and meaningful to the everyday lives of tutors, despite the fact that we don't really have time to think about them. The working life of the tutor is a busy one: full-time tutors teach a large number of contact hours each week with little enough time to prepare for sessions and mark assignments, let alone engage in speculation about the impact of market forces on the curricula that they teach. Part-time tutors sometimes juggle tutoring commitments with another job, or rush from evening class to evening class, juggling a number part-time fractional contracts in order to generate a living wage (I speak from experience on this matter!). There is no easy answer as to how it should be done, but finding some time to think and talk about the places in which we work is, I would suggest, a necessary first step in engaging with debates and concerns about the profession that we have chosen. I hope that this book has provided an accessible repertoire of issues and ideas around which a more sustained conversation about our working lives can be developed.

Index

accountability 16-17, 60
  and codes of practice 26
  and continuing professional
    development (CPD) 37
accreditation of prior experiential learning
  (APEL) 97–8
adult education tutors 67
adult learning, models of 83
Adult Learning Inspectorate (ALI) 15
Adult Math Project 84
andragogy 83
appraisal meetings and reports 42
Association of Accounting Technicians
  (AAT) code of practice 25
assumptions 75
audit 16, 60
  tutors and the culture of 17-19
autonomy, learner 88-9

Becoming a critically reflective teacher 75
behaviourism 82
being professional *see* professionalism
Brookfield, Stephen 75, 76

case studies
  codes of practice 28, 29
  preparing for a lesson observation 17-
    18
  professional tutors 6-9
  reflective practice 70-1
  staff appraisal 52
  tutors as managerialist or professional
    63-4
  widening participation programme 96
  see also journal extracts
class sizes, and professionalism 20
Code of ethical practice (Register of
  Exercise Professionals (REPs)) 25
codes of practice 22-32
  Association of Accounting Technicians
    (AAT) 25
  case study of complexity 28-9, 30
  function 31
  IfL 24-5
  problems 29-30
  rationale 25-9

Register of Exercise Professionals
  (REPs) 25
cognitivism 82
collaboration 46-56
  definition 49
college management, working with 51-4
colleges *see* further education colleges
collegiality 46-56
  definition 49
communities of practice 85
community-based adult education courses
  14
conferences, attending 41
continuing professional development (CPD)
  33-45
  activities and strategies 40-3
  identification of needs 40
  and the IfL 43
  and part-time tutors 43
  planning and preparing 37-40
    journal extracts 37-9
  rationale 34-7
    for colleges 36-7
    for teachers 34-6
  role 33-4
  and the Standards Unit 43-4
course managers 52
courses of action, justifying 58
critical lenses for reflection 75, 76
cross-college training days 39, 41
curriculum, changes to 34-5
curriculum managers 52

Department for Education and Skills (DfES)
  14-15
  and continuing professional
    development (CPD) 36
Dewey, John 73-4, 76
differentiation 92-3
  definition 93
disabilities, learners with *see* learners with
  disabilities
Disability Discrimination Act (DDA) (1995)
  35
  Part Four (2003) 98
diversity in the learning and skills sector 1-2